PRACTICAL BRITISH LIGHTWEIGHT FOUR-STROKE MOTORCYCLES

OTHER BOOKS BY THE SAME AUTHOR:

Practical British Lightweight Two-Stroke Motorcycles

British Motor Cycles Since 1950

PRACTICAL BRITISH LIGHTWEIGHT FOUR-STROKE MOTORCYCLES

STEVE WILSON

First published in 1994

British Library Cataloguing-in-Publication Data:
A catalogue record for this book is available from the British Library.

ISBN 0 85429 901 7

Library of Congress catalog card no. 93-80181

G. T. Foulis & Company is an imprint of
Haynes Publishing, Sparkford, Nr. Yeovil,
Somerset, BA22 7JJ.

Typeset by Character Graphics, Taunton, Somerset.
Printed in Great Britain by Butler & Tanner Ltd, London and Frome.

Contents

Acknowledgements

For their assistance the author would like to thank Steele Finlay and Dennis Frost of the LE Velo Club; the inimitable 'Tiger Cub man', Mike Estall; and Tony Jones of OTJ for painstaking work checking the BSA unit singles chapter. For the photographs, grateful thanks again to Cyril Ayton at *Motor Cycle Sport* and Frank Westworth of *Classic Bike Guide* as well as to Jeff Clew for the best LE pictures; and it's a double thank you to Jeff, because this little series was all his idea to begin with. Thanks also to Tim Holmes and Rebekka Smith of *British Bike Magazine*, in which a version of the true story "Me and my B40" first appeared. And finally thanks to a very long-suffering editorial supremo, Darryl Reach, who patiently bore an unusual number of delays as I fended off the slings and arrows while trying to get this one wrapped up.

Big man on a little motorcycle. Author Steve Wilson tests a long-suffering T20 Tiger Cub from 1965.

Chapter One

Starting out

What this book is for

This book intends to help you choose an old British four-stroke motorbike. The machines we consider are from the budget end of the market, yet hopefully ones which can be reliable enough to be used on today's roads on a regular basis. You may be new to motorcycles; or already involved with them and in need of a utility second machine; or returning after a long lay-off. But if you want a four-stroke British machine which weighs not much more than 300 lb, there should be something for you here.

In the end, of course, the decision about a machine is yours, based on your particular needs and preferences. There is a proverb that states, 'In choosing a wife and buying a sword, we ought not to trust another', and it could well be extended to buying a motorcycle, and particularly an old one. But we hope that some of the data and opinions which follow will help to make your choice a more informed one.

A basic definition. As you'll probably know, 'four-stroke' refers to the 'suck-squeeze-bang-blow' engine cycle, as opposed to 'two-stroke' which, as the name implies, fires each time the piston has gone up and down. Two-strokes are dealt with in the 'prequel' to this book, *Practical British Lightweight Two-Stroke Motorcycles* and are the ones that whir and scream, and on the British examples their oil is mixed in with the petrol. Four-strokes sound nicer and make less smoke. But their engines are also more complicated, and they tend to cost more both to buy and to run.

Which leads us to the next area, the budget. Our budget considerations are the purchase of a machine plus the cost of getting it on the road (excluding road tax, licences, test and training fees, etc). Whilst in 1989 it seemed to me possible to do this with an old British two-stroke for £500, today (1993) with a four-stroke, realistically the cost has to double, I think, to the £1,000 mark.

The thought of shelling out a grand for the dubious privilege of bimbling around on a C15 may give older readers apoplexy, but when you consider that our budget allows around £200 for clothes and equipment, the vision begins to narrow. A roadworthy Triumph Tiger Cub or BSA B25 in reasonable condition is unlikely to be found for much less than £600, and a fully sorted one

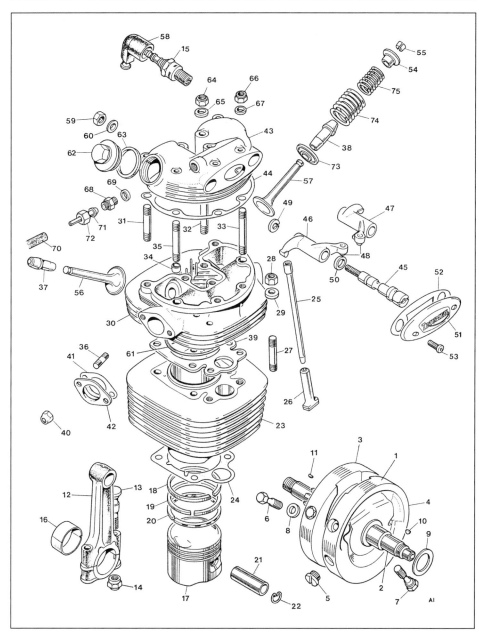

More bits than a two-stroke. Cylinder head, barrel and crankshaft from a 1969 Triumph TR25W Trophy.

could be around £800 or a little more. If you can do better, all well and good, and it's undeniable that the prolonged recession has had a steadying effect on prices, and that a low initial cost is the single best way to keep down the cost of a project. But I don't think you can rely on finding a bargain.

You can certainly pick up a rough or non-running machine in our category for £200–300, but if you want to use it then the serious spending begins. Even if you already possess a well equipped workshop and the engineering skills to go with it, the kind of basic items you are likely to need, though usually far cheaper than their Japanese motorcycle equivalents, do tend to mount up, and have also crept (or leapt) up in price over the last few years.

The following are some of today's approximate prices: decent tyres at around £35 each, plus £6 for an inner tube and another £1 for rim tape; £35 to have a seat recovered; around £20 for an exhaust pipe; £27.50 for a silencer; exchange brake shoes at £5, three or four control cables at a minimum of £3 each; a good rear chain at around £25; a rear number plate at around £10; a petrol tap at £5; and handlebars for £7. A non-runner may need many of these things, or maybe a pair of rear units at £45–75, a reconditioned speedo at £40 plus, or a wheel or two rebuilt at £35 a go.

Then there's those ever-troublesome electrics — light and ignition switches beginning at £10 and escalating way on up, bulbs at £3 a pop, a wiring harness from £15 or even an alternator at around £80. Almost certainly you won't need all, or even half the above items, but you can see how costs inexorably mount up.

If you're returning to or are already involved with the old bike game, you may have contacts or a useful cache of spares to help cut the shopping list. You can autojumble locally, you can save money and cover the seat yourself, you can lop £15 off the price of a tyre by fitting cheap Oriental imports (but I wouldn't), and there are more make do and mend tips to be found in Chapter Five. But you can do the sums yourself, and you'll note we haven't even mentioned the engine yet.

Once again, if you're a competent and preferably experienced mechanic you can save a lot of money, though large items which may need replacement, such as main or big end bearings and pistons, do not come particularly cheap. If you're not mechanically minded, in 1989 when I wrote the two-stroke book it was possible to get a full professional rebuild for a Villiers or Bantam engine for around £200. The same year I approached Tony Jones at unit BSA single specialist OTJ about a rebuild for a derelict TR25W Trophy 250 engine which had come my way, only to be advised kindly but firmly that the least a full rebuild on a unit 250 had ever been carried out for by OTJ was £600. There's just a great many more bits to fettle in a pushrod 250 four-stroke than in an equivalent two-stroke.

Note also that we're not talking about restoration, just getting the bikes running reasonably reliably and back on the road — that, and not restoration to strict originality, is what this book concerns itself with, though this is in no way a put-down of restoration with its particular skills and pleasures.

So by now the £1,000 budget for a four-stroke may begin to seem less exorbitant, and at the same time a guideline may be emerging, one good rule to keep the costs down. In the same way that Boy Scouts when firelighting are told to choose branches 'dead, but on the tree', I would definitely advise selecting a British lightweight which is 'rough, but on the road'. Not the dreaded 'basket case' or box of bits, not even the more seductive 'non-runner, needs slight attention', but a runner with an MOT (though sadly these can sometimes be less than a guarantee of anything), plus all being well some road tax and other evidence that it's been used recently and regularly.

Rough but on the road, Brian Pile's 1969 ex-police Velo LE (see True stories*).*

Why a Brit, and where to find one

I've written before of the triangle of dreams, needs and money which determine our choice of a motorcycle. With the exception of Velocette's little LE, none of the British four-stroke models we are going to consider could fairly be called 'classic' in the sense from the *Oxford Dictionary* definition, 'of the first rank', as opposed to the word's current commercial corruption, where 'classic' is used to describe anything which is simply old, or old-style.

There's nothing here as distinguished as there would be if we were considering European machines from the same era, BMW's R26 and R27, the 250 Ducatis and the NSU Max and Supermax. Yet for many of us the thought of a British motorcycle, almost any British motorcycle, has a unique appeal, compounded of nostalgia, individualism, plus a healthy regard for machinery potentially uncomplicated enough to work on oneself.

A four-stroke lightweight can be a relatively inexpensive way in to the 'classic' motorcycle scene, a way to share the dream, or the name on the tank at least, with the pilots of the Gold Stars and Bonnevilles, whom you may join at a later date when you're ready, or when money is a little less tight. As to needs, the machines selected all possess a benchmark 50 mph capability (though it's the top end for the LE), and are all potentially able to keep up with modern traffic.

Also these machines boast dry weights never more than a few pounds over 300 lb, and usually much less; they are thus suitable for riders of all ages and both sexes, not just muscular male enthusiasts. And with one exception (the B25/TR25W) they also possess pleasantly tractable engines, once again meaning that they're good all-rounders.

Another major consideration is that despite the quite high bottom line cost outlined in the previous section, the price gap with larger and more sought-after British motorcycles is real, and it does remain. (For the same reason, the lightweights we're concerned with are roadster versions only, since due to rarity as well as growing interest in pre-'65 trials and scrambles, machines like a genuine C15T fetch prices well above our budget.)

A well-sorted big four-stroke single comes in at around £1,200–1,500, and even the smallest Triumph twin, a 3TA or Tiger 90 350, in good order cannot usually be had for less. That leaves a gap of £400 to £700 with the price of a very decent Triumph 200 or BSA 250, and it is assumed that, for you as for me, a sum like that is not insignificant. And in today's light-fingered society, it's also a sad fact that these less cherished lightweights are less at risk from thieves than more desirable classics, something else which makes them a genuinely more practical proposition for everyday use.

On the positive side, once the bike has been purchased, British spares are available and cheap, with items like petrol taps and cables often costing much less than half of the Japanese equivalents. And once you've joined any of the owners' clubs, as well as a 10 per cent discount at some shops, insurance on an older machine offers really substantial savings — a year's fully comprehensive cover for around £65 is the norm with the excellent Carole Nash Insurance for a rider over 25, which can be a third or less than insuring a modern equivalent.

Another increasingly important concern now the £2.50 gallon is with us and the £3 one looming, is petrol economy. Any of these machines, even with inevitably worn engines and carburettors, should return at least 70 mpg and often 80 or 90, when most parallel twins are pushed to do much better than 50. In contrast to modern machines, however, this has to be balanced against the 3 to 5 pints of oil needed when you change it — as you will if you're wise — not much over every 1,000 miles; though there are real savings to be had here from buying in bulk from general suppliers or specialist oil companies like Penrite or Silkolene.

Finally, the price of a nice British lightweight machine will hold or even increase, in marked contrast to its Japanese or East European equivalent. (This argument is especially to be deployed when talking to a parent or bank manager.)

For the insurance savings alone, joining a club is a must. More discussion and information on this topic can be found in *Practical British Lightweight Two-stroke Motorcycles*. Here there is only space to say that the advice and help which clubmates can give will probably save you a lot of potential grief in all departments; and also that a club magazine's adverts can be a good place to locate a lightweight to ride.

Other sources of machine advertisements are the classic and motor cycle

press, bearing in mind that these relatively inexpensive machines are more likely to be located where advertising is either cheap or free. Your local paper is
always worth a scan. After that, starting with the obvious big weekly, *Motor
Cycle News*, other particularly likely papers are Ken Hallworth's *Old Bike Mart*
(a year's subscription is currently £4.85, arranged on 0298 815331), *Used Bike
Guide*, *British Bike Magazine* and, saving the best till last, *Classic Bike Guide*,
though here I have to declare an interest as the latter is the one I write for!

Which British lightweight?

This is a difficult bit. After the 'Practical Two-strokes' volume appeared, I got
stick about some of the machines which had been potentially eligible but
which I had considered should not be included, usually on the grounds of
'practicality' — in particular some devices powered by Villers engines whose
ability to generate forward motion was roughly equivalent to that of a Fairey
Swordfish biplane flying fully laden into a Force 9 gale. I stick to my selection
there, however, and will no doubt run into some of the same flak for the following. The criteria, apart from the higher £1,000 price already mentioned,
are the same — practical for this book means a 50 mph capability, the potential for reasonable reliability, and fair spares availability. Lightweight means not
much more than 300 lb dry at the outside.

The four-stroke Brits we consider in this volume begin with the charming
Velocette LE flat twin — they only just qualify for the 50 mph potential, but
they can be very reliable and have an excellent club spares back-up. Next
Triumph's Tiger Cub — not so reliable in many of its manifestations, but most

Left *One with universal appeal. A nice T20 Tiger Cub is bound to pull a crowd.*

Right *Sexy BSA for Swedish race car driver Yuge Rosqvist, who fitted lights on his 1962 C15T.*

can be made so and are true Triumphs in their lightness, liveliness and good looks. And finally the BSA 250 C15/B25, their badged Triumph TR25W/T25SS equivalents, and the 350 BSA B40, all expanded versions of the Cub which suffered from a poor reputation in the engine department. Often this was with good reason, but prices are low and spares are easy, and once again with selective buying and modern solutions, these BSAs can be a reasonably solid ride.

The first major exclusion is the range of unit singles from AMC, the AJS Model 8/Matchless G2, which were actually known as 'Lightweights'. But this was primarily to distinguish them from their 'Heavyweight' big single cousins, because weighing in at a minimum of 325 lb dry they were designed and styled as full-house middleweight motorcycles. Some 18,030 were built, including

around 3,000 350 versions, in nine years of production — less than a fifth of
Cub or Ceefer output — and both engine and chassis spares can be tricky. For
these reasons I have included no AMC lightweights, though they were quite a
nice bike, and cheap enough.

And for similar causes, there are no Royal Enfield Crusaders, the 250 whose
engine the later AMC bikes cribbed from heavily (same dimensions, same oil
carried in the crankcase). A bit lighter at 312 lb dry, nevertheless these hammering 250s looked and felt like bigger bikes. In over 10 years probably not as
many were made, in several variants, as even their AMC equivalents, though
spares are not too bad and they're a faster and relatively more robust machine.
A pity, then, but they're a little too rarefied to be practical, and not really lightweight in feel.

Also not included is a twin, Norton's 250 Jubilee. Though with some reser-
vations I am a fan of Norton's lighter unit construction twins, the Jubilee reliability in electrical and other departments was often not good at all, the cycle
parts provided only an adequate ride rather than what one expects from something with Norton on the tank, and the spares situation, never good, today is
chronic. I could add that they're well over our weight limit at 325 lb dry (335
for the superior 350 Navigator version), but the real barrier is psychological;
these machines were light twins all right, but a four-stroke parallel twin some-
how isn't a lightweight. So no Nortons (or 350 Triumphs, come to that).

No Brockhouse Indian Brave, either, the Southport-built side-valve 250 single being a desperately stodgy performer with a left foot gearchange, and being
mostly exported to the USA, today having a rarity quotient for both machines
and spares that practically elevates them to cult status. The same goes even
more so for the few Brave-engined Dots and OEC Apollos.

No Panther Model 65 and 75 250 and 350 singles. Quite heavy at 340 lb in
swinging-arm form, though worthy enough sloggers, they were and are once
again too obscure to qualify as practical today. The same could be said of
Ariel's 198 cc Colt single, a smaller, gutless version from within the BSA
group of Small Heath's C11G.

And here we edge onto the few exclusions I have to concede are indeed a little questionable. These are the side-valve BSA C10 and ohv C11, C11G and
C12, utility 250 singles all. They're mostly light enough — the plunger-sprung
C10L weighed only 256 lb and the swinging-arm C12 312 lb; despite being
machines for which the phrase 'grey porridge' seems to have been coined, even
a C10 could manage 50 mph on a good day, and several trustworthy BSA men
such as Owen Wright have a soft spot for the chuffing side-valve. Prices are
low and spares, while not on a par with the later mass-produced C15 family,
aren't bad. But... the head says that the early electrics, an old-style direct
dynamo and coil set-up with a car-type distributor, would be trouble, while
the 1953-on C10L and C11G, though featuring alternators, were also not
trouble-free, and the 1956-on C12 was flatly called 'a bodge-up' by BSA leg-
end and historian Norman Vanhouse. And the heart... the heart entertains
grave doubts about pointing anyone into the quagmire of British bike ownership along lines that are quite so uninspiring. So sorry Owen, no C10 or C11.

Of the machines we do feature, there is no one archetypal light four-stroke,
as there was with the two-strokes in the Bantam, and there's nothing completely bullet-proof. But there is something for everyone — the LE for those

Club outings can include trips abroad. Here in 1954 LEOC couple Fred and Doris Pickett from Birmingham are on their way to the Arctic Circle. Doris appears to have Fred on a leading rein, but is actually holding reindeer antlers!

seeking gentle commuting or touring, the Cubs for more flamboyant Triumph fans, the earlier unit BSAs mostly (if you're wise) for more middle-of-the-road requirements, the late oil-in-frame B25SS/T25SS for short-haul fun in town or on the trail, and the sports C25/B25 potentially for some quite serious, uncompromising road burning.

We can now proceed to the next three chapters and the engrossing business of choosing the budget machine which is right for you. It can be mentioned here that in these chapters where the machines are treated year by year, the book follows a factory practice which can be confusing if you are unfamiliar with it. Production generally shifted to the following year's model during August, so although, for instance, your machine may actually have been manufactured and even registered in, say, late 1959, it will be referred to in this book, as it was by the manufacturers, as a 1960 model.

After the chapters on the different models, in Chapter Five there are some hints, tips and addresses to help get and keep your British bike running. And then by way of some well-earned light relief, the final chapter gives two true-life stories of lightweights on the road.

Because the road is what it's all about — closing the circle, holding the line and keeping the ancient Brits and their battered but unbowed riders (of whatever age) out on the roads where they belong. And as a self-motivated (*sic*) forty-something failed hippie with two broken marriages and a weight problem, you can believe I take this *personal!*

Chapter Two

The LE Velocette

LE Velocette background

The LE Velocette calls to mind the title of a '60s song, *Strangely Strange (but Oddly Normal)*.

Conceived in a visionary way by Velocette's Eugene Goodman as clean, quiet and reliable transport for the masses (meaning people of both sexes and of all physiques and ages) the LE (Little Engine) was introduced for 1949.

It had a four-stroke, side-valve, horizontally-opposed twin cylinder engine (like a boxer BMW), with a forward-mounted radiator for its water-cooled cylinders and heads, and shaft final drive. A generator and coil ignition, then unheard of in lightweight circles, aided ease of starting. Noise was dealt with by the water cooling and by precision manufacture of the parts, particularly the primary drive gears, so much so that the loudest sound was sometimes the contacts snapping open and shut! Mess and weather protection were taken care of both by the design, which featured no chains at all and included no grease gun points, and by some inelegant but effective mudguarding, as well as by legshields, footboards, and panelling.

As well as protection, legshields gave a secure feeling of sitting 'in' the machine, which was one reason people would like scooters, and the footboards allowed the feet to be moved around to the optimum position. The very ample front mudguard combined with a chassis free of dirt-harbouring nooks and crannies and of mudguard stays, frame lugs, etc, to minimise cleaning chores. Comfort was built in by the sensational inclusion of swinging-arm suspension, adjustable for load, in Britain something merely Royal Enfield with their sporting machines and AJS/Matchless at the top of their range were only just offering, and something unheard of on a utility lightweight. And for servicing and repair convenience, the complete engine/transmission was detachable from the forks and front frame section, which could be bolted on later.

There were built-in pannier frames, plus a parcel/glove compartment where the petrol tank would normally have been located, in the main-frame 'backbone' pressing. Velocette had gone for a chassis design which, like most of the rest of the machine, could be produced accurately and in large numbers on automatic machinery.

1949, and Velocette Sales Director George Denley takes his place in the Birmingham traffic, imperturbable aboard the new 149 cc LE.

What aims did the LE embody for Eugene Goodman and the company? First, mass production was not to mean 'cheapness' in a throwaway sense, and the LE was intended to set standards that far surpassed anything else in the class; it was never meant to be the cheapest, but always to be good value for money. The innovative Velocette company had unswervingly high standards; as Titch Allen put it, 'an inability to settle for rubbish'. Unlike AMC boss Donald Heather, Eugene Goodman correctly assumed that the mass of the public would not relish spending their Sundays carrying out a decoke, and aimed at reliability, longevity and long intervals between major services — 20,000 miles without an overhaul was the stated aim, and if this sounds modest it was not, by the standards of the day. The choice of the well-balanced, horizontally-opposed layout of a four-stroke side-valve engine, and of water cooling, all contributed to an unstressed engine. Shaft final drive and gear primary drive did away with the expense and the chore of chain adjustment, as well as the mess. This lack of servicing was part of the good economy, a real consideration in those austere days of shortages and rationing.

It was also the reason behind the specially designed and very intricate seven-jet carburettor, which in good condition was intended to return 130 mpg, though it proved vulnerable both to dirt and to icing. The range given by the 1¼ gallon tank was intended to be that of a contemporary small car, and performance was meant to be in line with traffic conditions then prevailing, ie cruising at 40 mph with a top speed of 50 mph. Power should not be fierce enough for a non-motorcyclist to get into trouble, but there should be enough to carry a pillion passenger and climb any hill — though with the 150 cc Mk I even the factory had to modify this to 'almost any hill'.

The LE's smoothness and silence was a most striking feature, eliminating both a source of alarm for the new rider and of offence to the rest of the world. Despite the lack of an exhilarating exhaust note, and of engine noise to indicate whether it was labouring and time to change gear, it was a sometimes unexpected boon: you could ride out on a summer's evening and hear, as well as see and smell, the countryside. The silence was achieved by the rejection of the use of a two-stroke engine, by a collector-box beneath the main pressing, and by precision manufacture of the mechanical components. A final element in both the silence and the purring smoothness was that the pressed steel body could have acted as a sound box and amplified noise. So the engine was mounted on rubber to deaden vibration, and the inside of the pressed steel body lined with felt. In combination with the perfect balance of a flat twin and a non-snatch transmission, it all added up to the LE's characteristic smooth, purring gait.

Built-in luggage space in the shape of integral pannier frames and bags, plus a hinged glove compartment/toolbox forward of the petrol tank, with a q.d. (quickly detachable) rear wheel and a battery accessible by just lifting the hinged seat, and even a built-in licence holder, were among the other rider features. A glove compartment? Instruments, switches and an ignition light, all mounted dashboard-like on top of the leg shields? A radiator to top up? A car-type wet sump? A gear stick? All these give the clue to a strong theme of the lateral thinking involved in the LE: this was in some terms a two-wheel car, yet with full-sized wheels, the excellently rigid chassis and the exceptionally low centre of gravity, none of the motorcycle virtues had been skimped.

Seat height for the sprung saddle was just 28 in. Overall engine width due to the circular flywheel housing bolted to the front face of the crankcase, plus the deep setting of the cylinders with their width-reducing, side-mounted valve gear, was 14 in, almost the same as a Triumph twin, with the cylinders not protruding beyond the edge of the footboards, where they warmed the toes in cold weather. Kerbside weight at around 260 lb dry was reasonable, considering the water-cooling system and its $2\frac{1}{2}$ pints of lubricant.

These first LEs were implacably ingenious; Titch Allen has described them as 'an economy lightweight which ended up as the most sophisticated pure design in motorcycle history'. Novices find co-ordinating hand clutch and foot gear pedal operation difficult, so the Mk I LE adopted a hand gearchange lever with a car-type gate change putting neutral between each of three gears. Kickstarting with its balancing act and damage to shoes was eliminated by a hand start lever with a light pull. This lever also retracted the stand, which was in effect a pair of side stands, thus needing no effort to pull the bike on to them. Economy was also served by the thoughtful weather protection, since the expense (as well as the social stigma) of specialist clothing was avoided and the thing could be ridden to work in a business suit and walking shoes. The LE rider of whatever sex was expected to be a fully functioning member of normal society — George Beresford is seen in an illustration to his book, *The Story of the Velocette*, pootling down New Street, Birmingham, in a double-breasted suit and Homburg hat, while a lady in a summer frock loading up her LE with groceries is accompanied by the classic caption, 'The panniers of the Velocette turn drudgery into delight'. But in bad weather a suitable heavy coat was necessary, for there was one telling gap in this weather protection: the lack of a windshield. The reason for this probably lay in a problem area; the first

LE couldn't afford to lose the speed which a windshield scrubbed off because it was frankly underpowered, its 6 bhp 149 cc engine being less than ideal for a kerbside weight around 285 lb.

The inability to climb hills while carrying a pillion passenger became proverbial; indeed any gradients or headwinds slowed forward progress too markedly, and the 50 mph absolute top speed took too long to reach. The culprits were

Artist's impression of speeding along on an LE — but the public did not perceive it like that.

the lowly engine capacity and the choice of a side-valve engine, a layout usually producing 50 per cent less output than its ohv equivalent. There were also the almost inevitable teething troubles. The small engine was sensitive to even minor variations in ignition timing and carburation. The carburettor's tiny jets gave trouble, as did the BTH generator; the crowded roller big end bearings sometimes failed, leading to crankshaft failure, and on 'short run' usage, which after all was what it was mainly intended for, condensation within the cases led to failure of the ball main bearings.

Velocette reacted swiftly enough and by 1951 the LE, in Mk II form, had been bored out to 192 cc, as well as featuring a strengthened bottom end. Despite this and other problems being tackled quite effectively, unfortunately the wider public, who by definition were after utility transport at the right price, failed to appreciate the little Velocette's excellence of either rideability or design. Production problems delayed the launch and the price was very high for a lightweight, at £126, against £76 for a D1 BSA Bantam. The public wanted something cheap, cheerful and with an impression of zip, and orders for the LE never materialized in sufficient numbers to allow the small company to produce enough of them to enter profitability and drop the price, or to recoup fully the very high cost of tooling up for this truly different model. It must be remembered that everything, from the engine to the mudguards, the forks to the handlebars, the twistgrip to the carburettor, was special to this unique and unified design. An approximate total of 32,000 would be built over 22 years.

At 8 bhp the Mk II was still low on power and it was often said subsequently that expansion to the popular 250 cc class would have provided vital extra urge; but the design of the crankshaft, laid out to minimize the horizontal rocking couple, as well as the water-jacketing, determined that further expansion was not an option without major retooling, which the company could not afford.

From then on, however, the police orders began to come in, though special fleet discounts meant that the price paid to the company was less than the retail one. The police in more than 50 Forces nationally ended up taking over half of the LE's total production. The hard, high mileage the police LEs endured, with early Met machines having a life expectancy of 60,000 miles and being ridden on shifts round the clock, confirmed that the built-in longevity Eugene Goodman had intended had not been an illusion. 'They stood up well,' as a former Chief Engineer of the Met put it, and his counterpart in the Kent County Constabulary confirmed that 'They were liked by the riders, and the mechanics who maintained them had no difficulties', judging them 'ideal for their purpose' and 'the best lightweight motorcycle we ever had'.

Today LEs offer an often practical choice of British lightweight, but only with some important provisos. Despite the absolutely necessary back-up of a dedicated Owners' Club, for regular use a good degree of mechanical skill and sympathy is mandatory. The motor has been described as 'watch-like', and indeed the Pitmans manual advocates the use of a watchmaker's glass while setting and stoning the points! Ham-fistedness or impatience mean distortion and leaks from the water-cooling system. One UMG reader who inherited a clapped but willing LE found it refusing to run on one cylinder, so he took the plug out. 'When I spun the motor,' he wrote, 'there was a short squirt of water out of the plughole. I put the plug back in and off we went.' Repeating this procedure drew amused onlookers, though he also found that 'with careful positioning and a healthy kick, the water could be squirted with reasonable accuracy!' While long-lived and reliable, there are several points about LEs — a faulty dynamo, big end trouble — which the Pitmans book admits 'call for a visit to the expert' — who today doesn't exist, outside the club, that is.

Added to the LE's complexity is its 'sensible' level of performance and its almost aggressive normality. Len Moseley, a Hall Green man much involved with both the development and production of the LE, nevertheless recognized that 'the machines with the loudest exhausts are always more acceptable to younger riders', and with an LE, the silent side-valve, you abandon the element of motorcycling which roars around sticking up two fingers at society. This is probably all to the good, but the marginal power available on a well-used example, as most of them are, does tend to limit one to solo riding, preferably in town and flat countryside; epic trans-Alp journeys are possible, but only if you have a well-fettled machine and plenty of time.

Then there's the look of the thing. Beauty is in the eye of the beholder, but it would have to be a particularly myopic enthusiast who could deny that LEs are, frankly, ugly. This was a design fault; the Royal Enfield Airflow machines, for instance, show how a front mudguard could be both voluminous and relatively shapely. Leaving proportions and colour aside, although the LE is an enclosed machine there is still too much of the works and its plumbing still visible, and the clean handlebars were spoilt by the front brake cables snaking down outside the big front mudguard. One of the little Velocette's great competitors, Vespa, got this one right by shrouding the control cables within their stubby bars, just as they avoided Velocette's old-fashioned hand-change

Two-tone colour schemes and proprietary egg-shaped panniers, as seen on this Mk III, still fail to turn the ugly duckling into a swan.

solution to the problem for non-motorcyclists of co-ordinating clutch and gear pedal with a combined clutch lever/gear change on the bars — unlike the LE's car-type hand change, which meant removing your hand from the bars (and the throttle) each time. But the Velocette of course handled and held the road like no Vespa ever did.

As to colours, for their first six years it was 'any colour you like as long as it's silver grey'. The machine was born in the aftermath of war and in the middle of the age of austerity, appearing in 1948, the digits George Orwell would reverse to produce his vision of a grim, bleak cityscape in *1984*; an age when colourful display still seemed certainly frivolous and possibly indecent. Velocette would argue that grey matched the plating, conveyed the feeling of completeness, 'did not intrude in any surroundings' (very 'umble) and finally, as journalist and LE rider George Beresford observed in his little LE book, '...will not compete with the colour of clothing worn by the rider — a point of importance to women'. The overall appearance was more impressive in the first years, when the colour was polychromatic silver rather than plain silver grey, and the aluminium of the legshields was polished rather than painted.

But the fact was that the LE grey looked back to the warships of the recent conflict, when the world was already yearning for some brightness and gaiety, as evidenced by its acceptance of the cheerfully coloured European scooters. The company got the point in 1955, finally embellishing their panelling with nice little Velocette badges and offering two-tone finishes, much as their four-wheeled equivalent, the 2CV, would later do. But whatever you painted it, the LE was angular and ugly and through the 1950s and '60s grey always remained the characteristic LE colour. This was partly because it was favoured by the police. The force was responsible for the LE's nickname, the 'Noddy Bike'. I had always thought that this was due to the spectacle of PCs riding them wearing their regulation pointy helmets, or later varieties with thicker straps adapted into crash helmets, like Noddy's chum, PC Plod. But when I repeated this theory in print some years ago, a correspondent promptly let

A grim learner 'Noddy' is put through his paces by the Sergeant on a 1967 Mk III.

me know that 'the real origins have, thankfully, nothing to do with Enid Blyton.

'When commissioned for service by the Metropolitan Police, the new motorized constables, when confronted by officers of senior rank, attempted to give the customary salute. Now the manual clutch, gear change and throttle demand a level of dexterity beyond that of the average PC, so that when a salute was attempted many constables promptly lost control. Therefore it was agreed that a nod of the head would suffice as acknowledgment of the Chief Constable, a safer manoeuvre altogether!' As my editor at the time added, 'Even if it wasn't true, it makes a great yarn.'

The LE's silence conjured visions of police creeping up on malefactors but the truth was probably more mundane — the whispering twin was appreciated because it created no disturbance while patrolling residential areas after dark, and the public could talk with officers while its quiet engine was running. The days are gone when, as *The Classic Motor Cycle*'s columnist Rasselas described, clad in a black corker and long black mac, with the front number plate on the screen superficially resembling a 'police' sign, you presented a daunting figure in a motorist's rear mirror. 'As a way of getting to overtake anything on an LE,' Rasselas remarked, 'it was good. In fact, it was the only way.'

Some say that it was police pressure which led to the 1958 introduction of the foot-change, four-speed, kickstart Mk III. For Velocette it had been a case of Dr Johnson's remark about selecting the features of your work that you're most pleased with and then throwing them out. The ingenious stand lifter had already gone, and now so did many of the other 'Everyman' features, with the tiny carburettor giving way to a 363 Monobloc.

Eugene Goodman had taken charge of the company on his brother Percy's death in 1953, and there had followed various attempts to discover a successful variation on the basic LE formula, from the admirable but unsuccessful 1956 Valiant, an air-cooled ohv version of the flat engine in a conventional tubular frame, to the ill-judged 1960 Viceroy scooter with its horizontally-opposed 250 two-stroke engine and disastrously high tooling costs, to the LE-engined, fully faired Vogue, an Ariel Leader-style effort introduced well after the Leader itself had peaked, and one of which fewer than 400 in total were sold. It was the Valiant's foot-change, four-speed bottom end which went on the Mk III.

The Mk III is the practical LE and the one we shall be concentrating on. As LEOC historian Dennis Frost has pointed out, even Mk IIs were strong enough performers in their day, as proved by adventures like the 1954 trip from Birmingham to the Arctic Circle by Fred and Doris Pickett. But, as will be detailed later, problems with the Mk II engine were not fully sorted out until late in its life; and however apocryphal the 'Noddy' story, if the police riders had some difficulty with the hand change, the conventional route is the safer one. As the Pitmans manual puts it so succinctly, 'Four-speeds are better than three and a foot change is easier to operate than a hand control', going on to mention 'how much simpler and more positive both these controls are to work since at all times both hands can grasp the handlebars'. It made the LE, as a *Motorcycling* road test discovered, 'a far and away more pleasant motorcycle to ride' and gave it the realistic 50 mph performance we are looking for. With the Mk III, a final plus point came a little later, with the changeover after 1964 when the electrics altered from the 6 volt Miller to a 12 volt Lucas system.

Eugene (left) *and his brother Percy Goodman compare the first family expression of the 'Everyman' concept, a 1913 Velocette two-stroke, with the latest, a late-1948 Mk I production model.*

The LE is much more than one of motorcycling's oddities. Emerging from a factory known for its honesty of purpose, high standards and technical innovation, the little machine may have been aimed at those who would not normally ride a motorcycle, but it is nevertheless in many ways attractive to those who do, offering excellent handling and road-holding in all weathers from its flex-free chassis and very low centre of gravity, comfort from the layout, the rear springing and the engine's uncanny silence, and reliability from its shaft drive and mostly well-thought-out, understressed design. If one can live with its demands and performance restrictions, the LE is undoubtedly the quality option among British lightweights, and a uniquely satisfying machine to ride.

Velocette LE development history

Here is a short technical description of the original model, followed by the ways in which it was modified, up to and including the Mk III.

The LE engine, with its gearbox and clutch housing bolted to the back of it, and at the rear the drive shaft and its bevel box, all formed one unit, with the circular housing for the electrical equipment bolted to the front of the barrel-shaped crankcase. The two-throw crankshaft running fore and aft was of built-up construction. It ran on four main bearings, two ball races in a casting at the front and one ball race plus one plain bush in an outrigger plate, which Veloce called the reduction gear plate, in the crankcase rear wall. The two crankpins

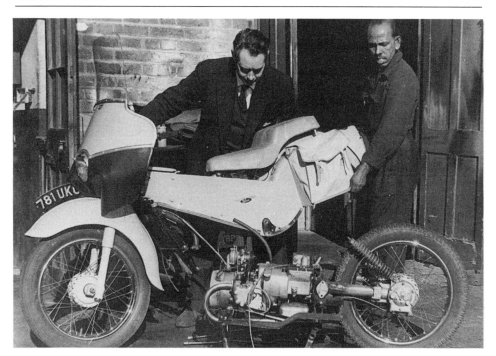

Mass production was facilitated by the way in which the engine/transmission could be joined or separated as a unit from the forks and 'backbone' frame.

were set at 180° to each other and formed in one with a centre disc. A bob-weight was a push fit on to each crankpin and then clamped into place.

Each narrow uncaged roller bearing big end, chosen to keep engine offset to a minimum, ran on a hardened and ground sleeve that was pressed on to the crankpin, with the 28 uncaged rollers running direct in the steel con rods. The small ends had bronze bushes and, due to their small size, to avoid reducing the bearing area the gudgeon pins were fitted with bronze end pads rather than circlips. The tiny Y-alloy cast pistons featured split skirts and three rings.

The cylinders were slightly offset in relation to one another. They were of cast iron with integral water jackets and, to reduce overall width, deeply spig-oted into the crankcase. Each one was retained by five studs and the top sur-face of each carried the valves. Also on the top, above the valves, were the inlet port and one pressed-in steel water hose connector; while the cylinders' front face carried the exhaust port and a second water hose connector. Both of the short, bright-chromed exhaust pipes ran back to a single, effective, square silencer box located beneath the engine's rear, with a single, short tail-pipe.

The cylinder heads were alloy, sealed with a copper-asbestos gasket. They were intricate castings incorporating water passages which connected with those in the cylinders. On the lower side of the head there was a drain plug and on the upper side, deeply recessed between the valves and screwing direct-ly into the alloy, was the small sparking plug, an unusual one in that it was a 10 mm plug with a long (12.5 mm) reach; the small size was to allow more effective water passages around it. The combustion chamber gave a 6:1 com-pression ratio and contained steeply sloping pockets into which the valves rose, creating turbulence. The combustion area was a circular platform above the piston, but proud of the surface and partly spigoted into the cylinder barrel so that the clearance between it and the piston top was minimal, and the charge was guided into position by the chamber's shape.

The valves were identical to each other and inclined to the bore. For both cylinders they were operated, via square section non-rotating tappets, by a single camshaft positioned along the engine above the crank. Beneath two squared-off access plates on the top of the crankcase, valve clearance was set by an adjuster screw in each tappet, locked by a nut. The camshaft was driven by a pair of spur gears at the rear of the engine within a timing chamber and ran on a pair of ball races.

At the rear of the crankcase, behind a bolted-on plate housing a support bush for the tail of the crankshaft, as well as a forward bush for the clutch shaft, lay the primary drive gears. At the crankcase front, between the two main bearings, the crankshaft carried a worm gear to drive the single gear-type oil pump. The pump was fixed to the main bearings' support casting and ran submerged in the oil of the car-type wet sump lubrication system.

In this system oil was held in a pressed-steel sump, which was fixed to the underside of the crankcase by 16 studs and sealed with a cork gasket. The screwed cap for the oil filler orifice was to be found on the left upper rear of the crankcase; capacity was just $1\frac{1}{4}$ pints (increased to $1\frac{3}{4}$ pints in February 1953). The sump carried a drain plug in one corner and a round mesh filter, held in place by a plate around the oil pump inlet. The oil went under pressure to a single jet beneath the crankshaft's centre web, which was cut away beside each big end so that oil was channelled approximately to each bearing surface. A pipe also took lubricant to the rear support plate and the plain main bearing there, as well as to jets to the camshaft gears and the gear primary drive.

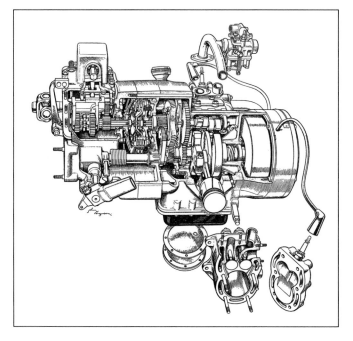

The LE powerplant — water-cooled, horizontally-opposed twin.

Splash and oil mist had to take care of the rest of the engine, which breathed via a chimney in the rear of the crankcase on the right, with a union and pipe at its top to remove overflow. This was the only external oil pipe.

At the front of the engine, after an oil seal, ran a flywheel in a compartment sealed off by the compact BTH three-brush generator unit. The unit incorporated all the electrics so that positioned around the crankshaft nose were the HT coil, distributor, ignition condenser and dynamo cut-out and the contact-breaker. This was operated by a single-lobe cam on the crankshaft nose, on early models via an automatic advance mechanism, though this was shortly dropped, and early ones could be locked in place. A single pair of points was operated by the cam, with a gear attached to it which meshed with the distributor above. A gap gauge was provided, clipped inside the housing itself.

At the rear the primary drive gears, which were helical for quietness, gave a 3:1 reduction to get clutch speed down and make the gearchange easier; and they moved the driveline out slightly, as well as up to the centre of the rear wheel. Behind the primary gears in a chamber separate from the three-piece gearbox housing, a conventional eight-spring, two-plate clutch ran dry. Within its housing the three-speed, all-indirect gearbox featured an input shaft coming in at the front and another alongside it and further out, which lined up with the rear wheel drive. The speedometer gearbox drive was placed vertically in the left rear corner of the gearbox and was driven by a skew gear splined to the output shaft. The two gearbox shafts ran in ball races and were connected by three pairs of gears selected by a car-type mechanism.

Immediately behind the gearbox was the universal joint, with its working centre on the pivot of the rear fork. The early Lay-rub joint's coupling was a disc with four rubber bushes bonded into it, with opposite pairs facing fore and aft. Flanges splined to the gearbox output shaft at the front and to the drive shaft behind mated with the disc's pins. The drive shaft then ran down the inside of the left rear fork leg to a light alloy bevel box bolted to the end of the leg, which housed spiral bevel gears giving a reduction of 3:1 as they turned the drive through 90°. The bevel pinion and the crown wheel shaft ran on two bearings each. Both had a needle roller bearing and the crown wheel shaft also used a conventional ballrace, whereas the bevel pinion also used a special split thrust bearing. Drive to the rear wheel was transmitted by a series of dogs. A high ratio permitted the use of a small bevel box.

The shaft drive's alignment with the engine clearly had to be perfect and this was achieved by the frame's support bracket, a substantial cross-braced steel pressing from which the stands were also suspended, with two rear-pointing flanges, both bolted to the rear of the gearbox. The flanges had holes in them to carry the pivot points of the fabricated rear fork, so alignment was fixed and the whole of the engine/transmission formed one easily detachable unit after eight bolts were unfastened.

The water cooling worked on the thermo-siphon principle without a pump or thermostat. The radiator, positioned between the legshields, consisted of one-piece head and bottom tanks which connected up the right and left latticed tube assembly. There was a release valve fitted in the top tank, and a filler cap, with gasket, on the left side. The radiator was connected to each cylinder by a pair of pipes. It was protectively mounted within a square tubular assembly bolted to the main frame, on rubber buffers. In the centre of the

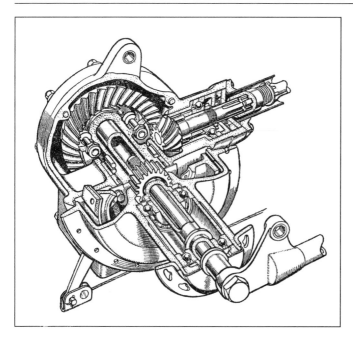

The final drive unit of the LE's shaft drive, mounted in the bevel box on the rear hub.

radiator was an enclosed space containing the air filter for the carburettor which, since it was fitted above the induction hose, pre-heated the filtered air.

The specially designed carburettor itself sat above the crankcase in the middle of a long induction tube curving down to each cylinder. Its bent wire cold start lever protruded from the left and only operated either on or off. The carburettor unusually also incorporated the petrol tap.

The engine and transmission fitted into a frame whose main backbone was an inverted U pressing of 22 gauge sheet steel, to which the wide rear mudguard was welded. At the front was bolted a welded steering headstock assembly with flanges pointing rearwards to mate with the main frame; the headstock contained the high-quality taper roller bearings on which the front fork pivoted.

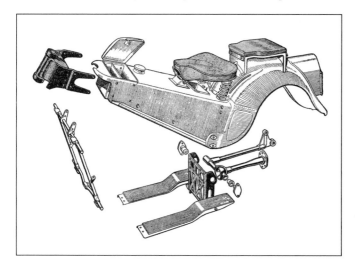

The 'backbone frame', headstock with flanges, tubular radiator frame, footboards and cross-hatched frame support bracket. Designed as a whole.

The engine was rubber-mounted to the main frame, with rubber bushes and washers at each fixing point. At its front, the top of the pressing contained a toolbox/glove compartment sunk within it, beneath a hinged lid embellished with a small Velocette badge and fastened by just a clip — no locks in those trusting days. Behind that, within the frame, was the 1¼ gallon petrol tank, and behind that a compartment into which to slot the battery, which as original equipment was usually the Varley non-spill type with jelly instead of acid. It sat beneath the Velocette's own sprung saddle, which hinged forward at the front to provide access to it; the saddle featured a sponge and rubber cushion with a detachable waterproof cover, and would stay in service to the end on the police models. A rather thin square pillion pad sat on the pressing above the rear mudguard, as if the manufacturers hoped you would use it as a luggage rack and not try the Mk I's capability to carry a passenger. There was more luggage space provided as standard in the pannier frames, complete with panniers, welded to each side of the rear mudguards.

At the front end the same tubular square that carried the radiator also supported the squared-off light alloy legshields. The shields carried the instruments and switches in their dashboard-like tops, with the speedometer on the left and on the right an ignition warning light plus switches for the lights and

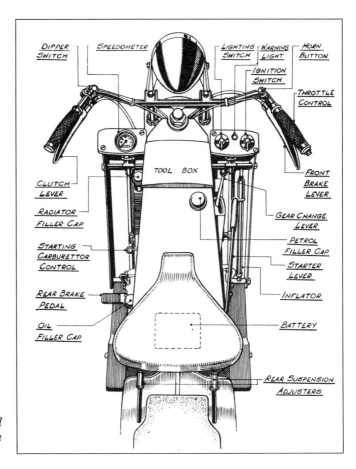

The Mk I's hand control layout was an acquired taste.

the ignition (the latter including an emergency start position), so that the 6 in headlamp was as bare as a bicycle's. A tyre pump was also clipped inside the right-hand legshield. The tubular assembly also supported the footboards, which connected to the bottom of the legshields and in turn supported the radiator's lower tube. The boards were stepped in the middle and covered in rubber matting; protruding from the left one was the pedal to work the cable-operated rear brake. Both the tubular support frame and the footboards themselves doubled as crash bars and protected the cylinders, whose mere 3 in protrusion stopped some inches short of the edge of the boards.

The swept back handlebars were another detail unique to the LE, being fixed and carrying both welded-on lugs for the headlamp and fixed pivot points for their levers. Controls were minimal, a dipswitch on the left and a horn button on the right, but even the twist grip was individual. As it was turned, a small brass block within it was made to travel down a quick spiral; the wire was gripped in the block, and instead of the normal winding action the wire received a straight pull.

The front suspension was by conventional telescopics with, carried between them, the electric horn, another striking 'extra' in those days which the LE offered as standard. The forks were oil-filled for lubrication rather than damping and carried the 3 x 19 in wheel on a leading axle. Around them was wrapped the machine's single least attractive but undeniably effective feature, a massive unsprung pressed steel mudguard, stayless and easy to clean, which carried a front number plate with a licence holder built into its rear end. The front tyre was ribbed, the early wheel rims alloy, and the front brake of

On the eve of the 1948 Show and the launch of the LE, Miss Myrtle Barrett demonstrates the hand starter. Note the silvery polychromatic finish, which lasted until mid-'51.

5 x ³/₄ in dimension, carried in an offset hub. Dimensions for the qd rear wheel and brake were similar, though the tyre was studded. The rear suspension was by Velocette's own units and inside were springs only, with no oil. The units were inclined forward and their top end, in a patented Velocette arrangement, was anchored in a long, curved slot in the mudguard; if the tops were loosened off, their position could be adjusted to suit the load, naturally the same on both sides, with the middle position being normal.

The new Mk I was finished in a polychromatic silver grey for the main pressing, front mudguard, handstart lever, front fork dust covers and the saddle bracket, with the alloy legshields and wheel rims polished. Only the headlamp rim, the gear lever and the exhaust pipes were bright chrome, with dull chrome for the top and bottom fork yokes and the fork sliders. Everything else, headlamp, handlebars, rear fork, footboards, steering head, radiator, all lower framing and the pannier frames included, was black. Dry weight was 260 lb. The engine produced a claimed 6 bhp at 5,000 rpm and on test the machine would return an all-out speed of 50 mph, with petrol consumption varying between 100 and 120 mpg.

Remarks

Before touching on the LE's teething troubles, it is as well to remember how much was right from the start. The water cooling system, the intricacies of the shaft drive and the gearbox were rarely to give trouble. Cycle parts worked very well, providing comfortable suspension, adequate braking and exceptional road-holding and handling, with cornering kept suitably sober by the claimed 5¹/₂ in ground clearance. The ease of starting, the silent smoothness, comfort and convenience were all as intended. It was a remarkable achievement.

The price of the engine's complexity was that although it was unlikely they would be needed until after high mileages, several service operations were also complex, needing special tools, so that a return to the factory was recommended for them. These included renewal of the flywheel housing main bearing bush, the crankcase main bearing bush housing and of the camshaft bush. A special tool was also needed to remove the BTH advance unit.

Of the design itself, the low power to weight ratio, as well as being a result of the use of side-valves, was to some extent due to the friction loss involved in gear and shaft drive. In the engine, early service problems centred on the complex carburettor with its tiny and easily blocked jets. The purpose-built BTH generator was equally fiddly to work on and there were problems as dust from its three brushes coated the internals.

Mechanically, the principal problems came about for two reasons. Some LEs suffered from lubrication problems, firstly as their moisture-susceptible ball main bearings fell prey to damage from condensation within the crankcase, when the machine was used for short runs only with long intervals of standing between them. The moisture would mix with the oil to form a sludge which could then cut off the supply from the singe oil jet to the mains and big end. Secondly, the big ends could wear prematurely, causing some crankshaft failures. Club researches indicate that the big end's uncaged rollers were a greater hazard to engine well-being than the condensation problems.

Otherwise, on the cycle side, the rear fork fabrication would sometimes eventually succumb to fatigue and crack. For the rider, engagement of the

The LE was a true non-sexist conveyance. Here is Mrs Ethel Denley of Velocette in a rural setting aboard one of the first production Mk Is.

light clutch could be abrupt, something aggravated by the difficulty of judging engine speed without the customary engine noise as a clue.

1950
There was little change for 1950.

1951
Saw the Mk I replaced by the 192 cc Mk II, with the Mk I's 49 mm stroke intact, but bored out oversquare to 50 mm, and with the engine numbers carrying a 200 prefix. The capacity increase was accompanied by internal strengthening.

The crankshaft was stiffened by means of the mainshafts now being forged integrally with the bobweights, and the crankpins being pressed into a taper interference fit. Both the big and small ends' diameters were increased, with the latter featuring an improved bush and the gudgeon pin now retained by a circlip. The cylinder head casting was machined to give more clearance volume and thus retain the modest 6:1 compression ratio. The tappets were changed from square to round section with flat feet which would rotate, and the cam profile was altered to give more rapid opening, yet retain the previous timing.

In the drive train stronger clutch springs were fitted. The rubber universal joint became Hooke type with Hardy-Spicer joint and needle rollers. There were detail changes in both the gearbox and the bevel box, where a spiral tooth formation was now employed, and second gear was raised from 13.0 to 10.85 overall.

In mid-year, from engine No. 200/11324, the lubrication system was changed. The pump's capacity was increased by 40 per cent with the fitting of wider gears and the crankshaft oil feed was revised, with the oil jet blanked off by a plug so that all the oil went to the reduction gear plate. This retained the bleed to the timing gears, as well as a pipe to carry oil up to fall into the clutch bearing housing. The principal oilway was now via the plain rear main bearing, into the rear mainshaft with, at the front end of the shaft, a restrictor jet in the bobweight. Thus oil was directed into a cup set in the centre crank disc, with oil holes from there feeding straight into the big ends. Just behind the restrictor jet the bobweight was drilled through and sealed by two washers, both held by a single central rivet, so that the crankshaft now incorporated a sludge trap.

From engine No. 200/12640 the BTH generators were progressively replaced by Miller AC3 counterparts, a process completed by the end of 1954, though the BTH was still listed until 1956. From the introduction of the first Miller electrics, the right-hand 'dashboard' was revised. The two previous switches were replaced by a single six-position ignition/light switch, still incorporating an emergency start position, with a detachable key which allowed the switch to be left in the off or parking light position, and the warning light was replaced by an ammeter.

The Miller AC3 was an alternator, with current controlled by an external half-wave rectifier mounted beneath the petrol tank, behind the carburettor. Thus inside the front compartment the previous distributor, cut-out and brush gear were eliminated. The ignition system was by coil, with a pair of HT coils mounted on the front of the stator plate, fired by the single pair of points opened by a points cam on the nose of the crankshaft, with an automatic advance/retard mechanism. Both plugs fired together, to give an idle spark. The Miller alternator was in fact unorthodox in carrying coils on *both* sides of the stator, as its three generating coils were mounted on the back of the stator, with the crankshaft-mounted rotor behind them.

The system was also unconventional for British machines at that time in being positive earth, and within months it was found that there was a danger of the battery being inadvertently connected up the wrong way round, which caused the rotor magnets to demagnetize.

On the cycle side there was an economy, with the taper roller steering head progressively being replaced by ball bearings, but with no discernible effect. Wheel rims became painted steel. All Mk IIs had grey steering heads and grey headlamp shells, and from May 1951 the finish was quietly altered from polychromatic silver to plain silver grey.

Mk II performance, while still limited, was definitely improved by the increase in output to 8 bhp at 5,000 rpm, particularly in terms of acceleration, tackling grades and carrying a passenger. Petrol consumption still averaged around 95 mpg, while top speed rose to 56 mph. After a slight modification, the Miller system improved on the BTH, though the points gap remained critical. The specified variation was 0.014 to 0.018, with the higher figure being the advisable setting in practice. While lubrication was improved, the bearing and big end problem remained for a while. The so-called colour scheme settled into drabness.

1952

In January, from engine No 200/15840 the Miller alternator became the AC3P, with a circuit-breaker built into the system to prevent the damagnetizing of the rotors if the battery was wrongly connected. The link between the stand and the starting handle was deleted.

- Capacious built-in pannier bags of stout waterproof material, provide accommodation for personal impedimenta.
- Light in action the hand starting lever automatically raises the prop stand before turning the engine over.
- Speedometer, and lights switch together with ignition warning light and a dual ignition switch are mounted in panels above the legshields.

For silent running, easy handling, and a clean means of transportation, the L.E. Velocette is without equal.

Combined footboards for rider and passenger, and rear suspension, adjustable for riding weight, make it an ideal "Two-up" mount, whilst ample engine capacity makes it possible to tour the most hilly country with confidence.

Inspect all the VELOCETTE models on STAND No. 76

THE SILENT L.E.

Velocette

Publicity for the Mk II 200, emphasizing hill-climbing two-up in an attempt to lay the Mk I's reputation for gutlessness.

1953

At engine No 200/19393 the rear brake shoe width was increased to 1 in. In the left flank of the main pressing a 2 in diameter hole, sealed with a rubber bung, gave access to the speedometer cable. From engine No 200/18975 the clutch was fitted with a third plate. From engine No 200/19609 a visible tell-tale appeared to signal important internal changes which were soon to follow. This was a cylindrical external oil filter, which bolted vertically to the front three studs of the right-hand cylinder. It contained a fabric filter and connected to the system via top and bottom pipes.

Shortly afterwards, at engine No 200/19917, the engine changed to plain main and big end bearings. Both were pressed-on fits, and oil holes were drilled through to feed all the working services. In addition a snake's pit of pipes was added in the sump, with the first taking the oil from the pump, which was unchanged, to a pressure-release valve bolted to the crankcase exterior beneath the right cylinder. There an adjustable valve let excess pressure back into the sump, while the rest of the oil was taken, via the filter, to another crankcase connection. The latter ran it to a distributor block in the sump, where three more pipes connected to the bearings and the reduction gear plate.

At the end of the year, from engine No 200/20344, the radiator's tubular frame was altered to make removal of the whole body structure easier. The lower cross tube was now a separate part from the two down tubes, connected to them by serrated split lugs and a bolt.

Remarks

The change in bearings and lubrication represented a major improvement, though not quite the final one, to engine reliability. Engines produced prior to this were often subsequently converted to plain bearings, usually for the big ends only, by the factory, which conversion will be evidenced by the presence of the external oil filter.

1954

The front brake came in line with the rear in now fitting 1 in wide brake shoes. From engine No 200/20253, the Miller alternator was changed to the AC4 type. This gave a higher output at 42 watts and added a ballast resistor in the supply to the ignition coils; at the same time the rectifier was changed to a full-wave type.

1955

There were changes to the cooling system, with the previous steel pipes and connecting hoses replaced by moulded rubber pipes to join the radiator with the cylinders. The bottom hoses were special, being flattened to clear the exhaust pipes, and the upper hoses had small outlets added to their rear. These connected to a cross-pipe welded to the carburettor's induction pipe, to heat the system and help prevent icing.

This year for the LEs two-tone colour schemes and other touches were added. The front mudguard, rear mudguard and lower edge of the main frame could be ruby red, green, or pale blue, separated from the grey with a black line. Velocette badges decorated the lower frame and chrome embellishing

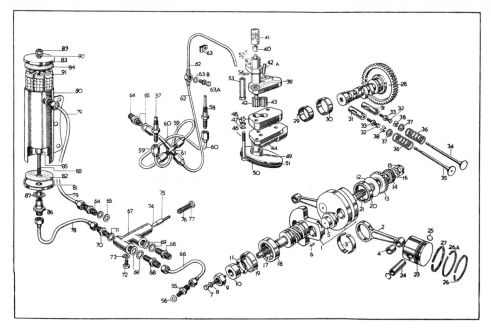

Plain bearing engine internals (from a 1965 engine).

strips were fitted along the lower frame edge, with plated trim from the rear pivot area to the edge of the rear mudguard.

Wheel rims became chrome-plated steel. A two-level dual seat with a pronounced step was offered, being pivoted at the front like the saddle, and where the pillion pad platform was retained it became a bolted on item. The rear frame was changed to take a revised numberplate, with its support now also a bolted on part rather than integral with the main frame.

From engine No 200/22046, the rear fork fabrication was changed to a stronger light alloy diecast component, which was left in its natural colour as opposed to its black-painted predecessor.

Inside the engine, from engine No 200/22637, the move to plain bearings was completed as the camshaft was modified to run on them, with the oil feed modified to suit, the camshaft now being hollowed to supply the front bearing. Soon after, at engine No. 200/22678, the rather narrow plain big ends were widened by $1/16$ in, which was permitted by making slight alterations to the flywheel housing and the crank cheeks.

Remarks

The restyling was in response to flagging sales and it is debatable whether it really suited the uncompromisingly functional LE with its untouched front end. Still, Velocette once again led the field, as it would be two years before most of the rest of the industry began to follow the scooters and go two-tone.

1956

The petrol tank capacity was enlarged from $1\frac{1}{4}$ to 1.62 gallons, though still no reserve was fitted.

As an option, a new design of rounded, egg-shaped metal pannier boxes was offered, though the old panniers and frames were still available. On the finish front, the legshields were now no longer left plain and polished, but painted

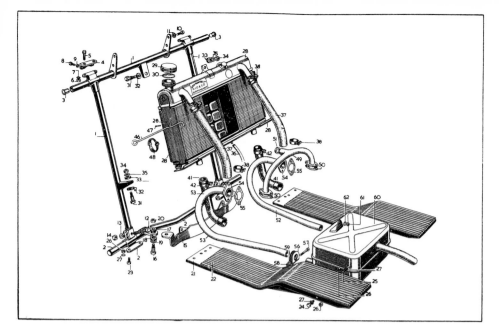

Final, post-1957 version of the radiator.

whatever colour the mudguards were finished in. There was an additional sub-dued two-tone colour offered, with dove grey for the guards, etc.

1957

Late in the previous year, at engine No 200/25503, the Udall carburettor was displaced by a Monobloc 363. Since this had its own integral strangler-type choke/air cleaner, the previous radiator-mounted air filter was deleted, with the radiator modified to suit. The fuel tap was repositioned conventionally at the top of the fuel line, in a threaded boss on the bottom of the petrol tank, with an extension bar on its operating lever poking through a hole in the left of the frame pressing.

Very soon afterwards, at engine No 200/25527, a further modification to the lubrication system took place. The sump was made deeper and became a plain pan. This was because the oil pump had been altered to incorporate a circular intake filter, so the sump's previous gauze filter and its access plate were no longer necessary.

At almost the same time, from engine No 200/25539, the LE's wheels and tyres, in line with current trends to smaller wheels, were altered to 3.25 x 18 in, front and rear and, fashionably again, the hubs became fully enclosed. An optional oil gauge, which the plain bearings permitted, was offered, fitted on the left in a revised legshield panel next to the speedometer. A fifth two-tone option in polychromatic deep olive green was offered. The handlebars for all became grey-painted.

1958

This was the last major change year, with the introduction at engine No 1001/3 of the Mk III. The location of the engine numbers themselves changed a little, from the area of the crankcase beneath the carburettor to the area behind it.

The change to foot gear shift, a four-speed gearbox and a kickstart (sorry,

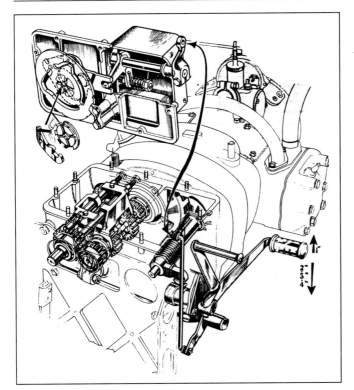

Four-speed foot gearchange introduced for 1958.

'starter pedal') all of course derived from the 1957-on tube-framed ohv Valiant. There was considerable commonality between the two models which from now on shared their crankcase, driving shaft assembly, flywheel housing assembly, crank, crankshaft, con rods, and crank disc assembly, gearbox, clutch, universal joint, bevel drive assembly, front and rear wheels, handlebars and fittings, forks, headlamp cowl and brackets, electrics, oil filter, oil distribution block and pipes, and even the tool kit. The Valiant had a greater offset between its cylinders than previous LEs, which Mk IIIs adopted. The only difference between Mk III and Valiant crankcases was that on the former the tappet inspection apertures were drilled out, but not on the latter. Also, a cast boss on top of the crankcase by the breather was drilled ¼ in BSF on the Valiant, to take the external oil pipe to its ohv rockers.

The kickstart, mounted above the gear pedal, was almost a straight replacement for the hand lever, though the kickstart lever shaft was of square section with the kickstart itself using a clamp fitting, while the handstart lever had been keyed and pressed on to a circular shaft. A positive stop mechanism was built into the gearbox lid and the frame body altered to remove the previous hole for the lever. The new four-speed gear cluster was compact enough to fit into the same space. The compactness was achieved by using a single row of dogs in the middle of the input shaft to drive both third and fourth, which were on either side of it. The fourth speed meant a round camplate in the top of the gearbox, connected to the positive stop mechanism, which had an external link running down to the pedal on the right. The gearbox casting was deep and the silencer was indented to match this: the pressing bolted to the rear of the gearbox was also altered, with four attachment bolts in place of the previous seven. The speedometer cable was relocated, now coming out of the front left-hand corner of the gearbox.

The petrol tank was moved slightly to the right to make room for the new speedometer arrangement, with the petrol tap and the access hole for it now also going on the right. The induction pipe heating connection was deleted, as the Monobloc had been found not to be so vulnerable to the cold. The carburettor was set square to the pipe to avoid induction bias, with the pipe itself angled to suit the cylinder offset.

The front brake plate was now spun over the rim to seal the interior of the drum and so waterproof it.

One welcome piece of styling adapted from the air-cooled model was the headlamp shroud, which fitted on the upper forks, shrouding them and the fixing points for the handlebars, which were a new shape with less of a rearward sweep than previously, before running forward to surround and support the headlamp shell. The latter now carried the speedometer as well as the ignition/light switch on the right and the ammeter on the left. The legshield 'dashboards' were thus no longer pierced, although the optional oil gauge could still be had, set in the left one. But with the cowl masking the area between the forks, the horn was now carried in the front of the right legshield and, to balance this, the special licence holder was deleted from the front number plate and fitted on the front of the left legshield. The dual seat was now optional, with the saddle standard. The previous straight-pull twistgrip changed to a conventional type.

In mid-year the LE followed the Valiant in changing the previous ball bearing in the oil pressure relief system to a plunger. It also fitted the Valiant's Ferodo bonded clutch plates, which were hardened by moving the edges of the driven plates and bell slots inboard.

In finish terms, the two-tone options were reduced to three: light willow-green, polychromatic deep green, or blue. The area covered by the colour no longer included the legshields, which from now on were always silver grey with polished alloy tops.

The Mk II continued to be listed until October 1958 for true believers and around 100 were sold that year, with single figure numbers going out to special order until 1962, as well as a few three-speed Mk IIIs.

Remarks

The new four-speed version was welcome, as the hand change had only been liked by a minority, and it represented another step up in performance. Although its output was unchanged, testers found the machine could now be revved through the gears to around 40 in second and 50 in third. Engine braking was also improved by the operation of the foot-change gearbox. With the conventional layout and carburettor the LE might be less of a concept made metal, but it was now an extremely effective light motorcycle capable of very high trouble-free mileage — round the clock was far from unknown. It also looked better, with the headlamp styling, nodding in the direction of the Triumph nacelle, ending the era of the protuberant headlamp with its air of a superannuated moped.

Left *Full-dress police Mk III for the Hertfordshire Constabulary, with high output generator for extra electrical equipment, and 'Big Ears' Olicana windscreen.*

Right *Mk III. Note the improved headlamp arrangement.*

1959

Windscreens had been available since 1955, the Olicana being the most common but, possibly in response to the four-speed's brisker character, a new one was offered as an option. With its protuberant sections protecting the handlebar grips, on police machines its silhouette was more Big Ears than Noddy. Also early in the year, at engine No 2166/3, the piston rings were modified, with an increase in their radial thickness.

1961

The headlamp rim was modified and a stop-lamp became optional, while the egg-shaped panniers no longer were.

From then on, a great majority of LEs went to the police, for whose use they came equipped with a larger generator and a Miller two-way radio telephone.

1963

On the feet of the centre stand, small U-shaped extensions were added. With the 18 in wheels, both tyres touched the ground when the machine was parked on the stand, and the extensions were to prevent it 'running off' the stand if left facing downhill.

As a result of police requirements the last major update came about, commencing in the middle of...

1964

Mid-year, at engine No 6555/3, the electrics became a 12 volt Lucas system with either twin 6 volt batteries or one 12 volt, and a 90/100W RM19 alternator. Its twin ignition coils were now mounted behind the carburettor and the output was controlled by a Zener diode bolted under the toolbox/glove

compartment. The two switches were new and moved back on to the right-hand legshield top panel; an ignition switch still with an emergency start position and removable key to the right, and a light switch on the left, with the ammeter between them, leaving the speedometer still in the headlamp.

At the beginning of 1964 the cylinder head had been re-designed with the water passages reduced from five to three, which led to some casting problems.

1965

This year saw both the engine and the chassis strengthened. The barrel castings were revised to modify the water passages so that the gasket area around them was increased. Behind the gearbox the propeller shaft was waisted to increase transmission flexibility. The oil feed into the crankshaft was increased, the timing gears were widened and in the bevel box a stronger crown wheel and a pinion with larger teeth of thicker form were fitted. The carburettor changed to a new Amal type 19/5 Concentric, with a slightly increased bore. The frame pressing changed to a heavier gauge and a heavier rear brake pedal was fitted, incorporating a right-angled toe-guard to protect the Bill's bulled-up boots.

1967

Further stiffening was added to the underside of the frame body. In finish terms an all-black option was added for police use. Colour schemes were specified by the ordering Force — Lancashire, for instance, specifying Maroon.

Remarks

That was the end of LE development, and the '65-on strengthened machines with more powerful electrics must surely be desirable, although this must be

The end. Journalist the late Bob Currie (right) on 3 February 1971 watches with Velocette company secretary Tom Chivers as the last completed machines, Mk III LEs, leave the assembly line.

balanced against some evidence of declining build standards at the factory from the late '50s onwards, as the wages Velocette could afford to pay failed to keep pace with the national average and skilled labour drifted away. But the main customers, the police, were happy enough with the LE. When the end approached in 1970, Kent County Constabulary, despite the onset of vans and Panda cars, bought up over £11,000 worth of spares and with them, and some improvisation and cannibalization, kept their remaining LEs in service for a further seven years. Their high regard for the machines which outlived every other type of light motorcycle they had put into service is eloquent testimony indeed for the LE from the real, hard world.

The LE Velocette Mk III today

In most big towns, if you stick around long enough, you will spot the regular LE rider on his way to work and back. He can often be distinguished by his old and fiercely utility riding gear, an antique crash hat, plus round National Health spectacles, as well as by the mildly aggrieved air of a man who, as they say in Norfolk, 'do different'. Usually in his late middle years, he steadfastly ignores the attention his steed attracts, either from people who have latched on to British bikes as part of the heritage industry, or who are simply struck by the machine's quaintness — it is, after all, rather like a child's drawing of a motorbike. His unspoken attitude is that the thing has been getting him about for many years and, looked after properly, which he can assure you it is, why shouldn't a machine which was correctly conceived and constructed in the first place carry on for as long as he needs it? And what's special about that? The LE, in other words, is to him the living refutation of Dr. Johnson's proposition that 'nothing odd will do long'. One double irony is that while a relatively high price told against the LE during its production lifetime, today it is the most affordable of British classics, as riders shy clear of its modest performance and complications. Around £300–£500 can secure a good running example, with a great deal less for a non-runner. They are also cheap to run, with the good mpg intact and spares where available very reasonably priced. Valiants, on the other hand, and ironically in view of their sales flop, are now sought after, starting around £700, with the very best examples fetching up to £2,000. Ironically again, Spares Secretary Steele Finlay once bought for a fiver a Hong Kong-made toy LE with a police rider. Recently an American collector paid £700 for a similar one!

Yet despite the cheapness, an LE is not an ideal choice for a first rebuild. The fluctuations of membership in the 800-odd club bears this out, with 180 incoming and 150 outgoing subscriptions in 1988, most of which represented those who bought an LE as a first rebuild and had joined, attracted by the deductions from spares' costs. Then they lost heart when confronted by the fact that this is an engineer's machine — you don't buy big end shells for it, you get lead-bronze bar and machine them up yourself.

If buying an LE, points to watch are cracks around the rear suspension mounting slots and rusting of the double skin underneath the saddle. Frame buckling around the toolbox will indicate crash damage. Roller bearing engines may well need converting to plain big ends. On the plain bearing engines, oil pressure should be checked — 30 psi should register at 30 mph in top gear when the engine is warmed up. These tips come from club historian Dennis Frost and, even more than is usually the case, there is really no substitute for taking along a knowledgeable club friend when prospecting to buy an LE. If you're repainting, an approximate equivalent for Polychromatic Silver Grey is Ford Silver Fox Metallic, and though there is no close equivalent to the plain grey, Austin-Morris Farina Grey is a reasonable match.

As indicated, several aspects of working on the engine require both specialist knowledge and specialist tools. The only source of these today is the owners' club and specifically Jeff Tooze, who has organized the necessary special reamers for the main and camshaft bearings. He offers a reconditioning service for bottom ends (plain bearings only, though earlier bearings can be converted), or will rebuild whole engines for around £250 or, indeed, restore entire machines. If you are carrying out other service tasks yourself, the club offers the loan of special service tools. The Technical Secretary will also provide advice.

Running an LE today means in fact reliance on the club as well as yourself. They are a happy band with their own three-storey clubhouse in Bradford Lane, Walsall, restored by the membership themselves and known as The Premises or Buller's End. The latter derives from a fictional West Country village, complete with Charlie and Maureen the barmaid, whose goings-on are described from time to time in the club mag, *On The LEvel*, by the quirky

The photograph taken when the news about the new LE model was first announced in Birmingham; and a club gathering at the same venue 40 years on.

correspondent 'Delocette'. Buller's End houses the club's stock of spares, which are dispensed to members at a counter on Wednesday evenings, as well as worldwide by mail order, including to the club's active Japanese section. This is just about the only source now; even dealer Roy Smith gets some of his stock from them. The club started buying up both new and secondhand spares some while ago and now has many manufactured by itself, experiencing the cares of gauging quantities and delivery time which, like demand, can be unpredictable. Most members appreciate this, as well as the voluntary basis of the services provided, and only a few will moan if their order isn't filled in five days flat.

The gaps the club has filled have sometimes been crucial. The rubber in the mounting bushes perishes, for instance, and this was a significant problem since when it happens it contributes to heavy transmission wear. Past Technical Secretary, Dr David Rix, discovered the significance of this through extensive road-testing, and the club now recommends that new washers and buffers are fitted at each major rebuild. (New stocks of these items have been produced.) David Holder, the inheritor of the Velocette name and bulk manufacturer of British spares, has been very helpful in supplying original drawings and is currently manufacturing some components for them.

There are real problem areas, and the early BTH electrics is one of them as they are not easily convertible to later spec, though the factory did so in some cases. This can only emphasize the later models as the practical choice, with the Lucas RM19 alternators being the same as those fitted on some unit Triumph twins, and with the same ATD unit. Points for the Miller stator plate, however, have dried up, so the club offers a conversion to accept Lucas Ford Cortina points. Miller generator flywheels can also be remagnetized. Miller electrics are thin on the ground generally and Lucas or Wipac headlights are regularly substituted. Other club services offered, incidentally, are cylinder head skimming and oil pump overhaul. Despite the problems, in recent years there has been increasing interest in the older machines for restoration, where previously the concern of the majority was about machines, often ex-police, which were used regularly for commuting.

1954 MkII — not so practical, but a favourite with restorers today.

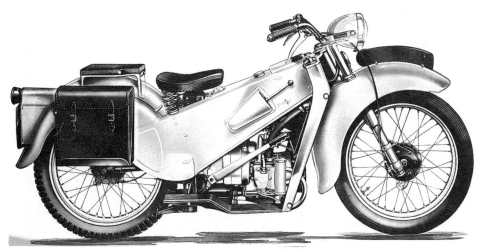

These are our meat, so for those not too concerned with originality it will be interesting to see if a Concentric carburettor substitute will be found or whether the depth of the inlet stub will prove it unsuitable. Another problem can be the rear suspension units. Substituting Girling units is not ideal, due to the different type of top and bottom fixing. Some have used Girlings and Littlejohns used to offer something suitable, but this altered the frame geometry so that the swinging-arm was no longer horizontal. The club has had the unit's plunger tubes made, but is still looking for a substitute for the original moulded Oilite bushes. Graphited nylon was tried, but that tends to absorb moisture, expand and seize. You can have 250,000 new Oilite bushes made — but not, economically, just 1,000. And so it goes. It is also important to keep dirt out of the spring unit by covering it with some kind of gaiter; police LEs had one as standard.

Even more mundane items can be difficult. The later 3.25 x 18 in tyres are a problem, since there was always only limited clearance with them, and modern ones, with their rounder section, foul the mudguards. The answer seems to be Chen Shing Far Eastern imports, which are used by some Valiant riders (in both senses?) and are the only tyre of those origins which Steele Finlay will countenance. The 10 mm plugs with 12.5 mm reach (Champion Z-10 and today NGK/C7-HS) are unusual enough to be worth hoarding a few. Real 'unobtainia' include the upper water hoses with the heated induction take-off (the club does all other hoses); the correct 10/12g butted wheelspokes; and the unique six-position switch for Miller electrics.

Changing a plug, as indicated, has to be done with care, due to the proximity of the water passages — broach one by cross-threading or over-tightening and it's a matter of a new head, if you can find it. Graphite grease on the plug threads is recommended. Not all the maintenance work is taxing — the eight-spring clutch, for instance, is easy enough to adjust. But the brakes, good enough but never brilliant, need careful attention to make sure that shoes and drums are in good condition and that the unique packing shoes

which go under the slippers are correctly adjusted. Among other points to watch are oil changes, which with the tiny $1\frac{1}{2}$ pint capacity have to be made religiously every 1,000 miles if the oil is not to turn into an emulsified mess; the box silencer, which tends to build up a coke deposit that then has to be burnt out of it; and the sealing of the head to barrel joints, which can be troublesome.

Starting an LE is not always a first-time affair and, like starting a Triumph though for different reasons, benefits from a few kicks after turning on the petrol but *before* switching on the ignition, to help prime the long induction passages. In hot weather, or under heavy load, a fuel lock may develop in the petrol pipe, which can be cleared by removing the fuel filter and blowing. As mentioned, the points gap should be on the generous side, though if too large it makes for difficult starting, while too narrow causes intermittent firing while pulling uphill. LEs ran best on two-star petrol but now that's gone it's four-star; unleaded petrol is not recommended, because of the risk of premature valve seat erosion.

Otherwise, typical riding experience can be found described on p.171 in Chapter 6. Just riding an LE rather than fettling it is an easy experience to relish, fun and satisfying and, before getting too intimidated by the pitfalls, it's worth remembering the little machine's certified potential longevity, as well as a remark by the heartless UMG reader: 'The LE turned out to be one of those bikes that could be caned and caned without exploding.'

In parting, I'll pass on my one piece of LE tuning lore. I overheard it at an LEOC stand at a classic show and passed it on to my LE riding pal, who verified it on his ex-police machine in the metal. It seems that on some police Mk III machines, on the underside of the twist grip there is a small screw. Remove it and you gain about an extra third of a turn throttle, with performance increasing to match. (Some police LEs also had 'long' throttle valves in the carburettor, also to restrict performance.) Strange but true, which seems a fitting keynote for the LE itself.

Velocette LE Mk III (1958): Technical Data

Engine

Bore (mm)	50
Stroke (mm)	58
Capacity (cc)	192
Compression ratio	7.1:1
Ignition	Coil
Carburettor	Amal Monobloc 363

Transmission

Top gear	7.3
3rd gear	9.8
2nd gear	13.3
1st gear	20.4

Brakes

Diam front (in)	5
Diam rear (in)	5

Tyres

Size front (in)	3.25 x 18
Size rear (in)	3.25 x 18

Electrical

Battery	8 ah
Headlamp (diam in)	$6^{1}/_{2}$
Voltage	6

Miscellaneous

Fuel, (Imp. gals)	$1^{5}/_{8}$
Seat height (in)	28
Width (in)	25
Length (in)	82
Ground clearance unladen (in)	$4^{1}/_{2}$
Dry weight (lb)	263
Speedometer	80 mph

Engine and frame numbers

Start year numbers are not available for the Mk IIs in the 1950s, so some of the relevant numbers when changes were introduced are included, with the months they occurred, to give an approximation.

The LE's frame number was on a plate riveted inside the lid of the toolbox/glove compartment, or on the left-hand steering head in the case of some police models. With the passage of time either will sometimes be missing. The Mk I and Mk II engine number was found on the crankcase beneath the carburettor, though from about 1955 it was also included on the toolbox lid's plate. The Mk III engine number moved further back on the crankcase, behind the carburettor.

Mk I's engine and frame number should be close to one another if original; there were four numbers each for engine and frame, starting at 1000, ending around 8500. Mk IIs start at 200/1001, and an original engine number will be around 1500 higher than the frame. Mk III's numbering goes back to four main figures, with a /3 suffix for the engine and a /34 suffix for the frame, starting at 1000/3 and 1000/34. The four figure numbers will usually be identical if original, but if a Mk III engine went in a Vogue there will have been no LE made with that frame number, so there are gaps from 1964 to 1968. Also many ex-police LEs will have had an engine swap.

Year (month)	New feature if any	Model	Engine	Frame
1948 (Nov)		Mk I	1001	1001
1950		Mk I	6374	6393
1951		Mk II	200/1001	8500
1952 (Jan)	Miller AC3P		200/15840	14378
1953 (May)	Three plate clutch		200/18975	17523
1953 (Nov)	Radiator frame mod		200/20344	18878
1954	1 in wide front brake		200/20992	19251

Year (month)	New feature if any	Model	Engine	Frame
1955 (Feb)	Plain bearing camshaft		200/22637	21550
1955 (Nov)	Chrome piston top ring		200/24439	22956
1956 (Oct)	Monobloc		200/25503	23967
1957			200/26083	24689
	Ends	Mk II	200/27395	25884
1958		Mk III	1001/3	1001/34
1959			1954/3	1954/34
1960			2992/3	2992/34
1961			3958/3	3958/34
1962			4681/3	4681/34
1963			5271/3	5271/34
1964			5985/3	5985/34
1965			6800/3	6800/34
1966			7523/3	7523/34
1967			8030/3	8030/34
1968			8592/3	8592/34
1969			8720/3	8720/34
1970			8962/3	8962/34
1971 (Feb)	Ends	Mk III	9071/3	9071/34

LE Useful Information

Books

Velocette Flat Twins by Roy Bacon (Osprey)

Always In The Picture by Jeff Clew and Bob Burgess (Haynes) Marque history.

The Story of the Velocette by George Beresford (G.S. Davison, o/p)

The Book of the Velocette by Ferrers Leigh (Pitmans, o/p) Half of it is on the LE.

Velocette by R. W. Burgess (C. Arthur Pearson, o/p) A chapter on the LE.

My Velocette Days by Len Moseley (Transport Bookman, o/p) Memoir by a Velo foreman, including production details on LE.

Technical Notes on the Maintenance and Overhaul of the LE Model by the LE Velo Club, available to Club members only.

Clubs

LE Velocette Owners' Club, Membership Secretary: Peter Greaves, 8 Heath Close, Stonnall, Walsall, West Midlands WS9 9HV. Eligible for VMCC insurance scheme.

Shops

Roy Smith Motors, 116–24 Burlington Road, New Malden, Surrey (Tel 081 949 5731).

Dave Mac Propshaft Services, 1–3 Northey Road, Foleshill, Coventry CV6 5NF (Tel. 0203 683239). Suppliers of universal joints for LE shaft drive.

Jeff Tooze, 32 Mackie Avenue, Bristol. Engine rebuilds etc (see text).

Martyn Bratby, P/O Box 6, Burntwood, Walsall, West Midlands WS7 8NZ (Tel. 0543 71250). Amal 363 carburettor gasket sets.

Chapter Three

The Triumph Tiger Cub

Tiger Cub background

In 1953 Meriden publicity called Triumph's Terrier, forerunner of the Tiger Cub, 'A Real Triumph — in Miniature!' That would remain true of this little four-stroke single for the following 15 years of its life.

Triumph's presiding genius Edward Turner dictated that, like his twin-cylinder market leaders, the bike should be light, lively and low, not only in price and running cost but also in seat height. Turner himself was no giant, but more significantly, like Velocette's Eugene Goodman, he had long cherished a vision of two-wheeled transport for everyman — which notion included, to his credit, something usable by people of both sexes and all ages and sizes. So Harry Summers, Turner's chief draughtsman at the time, and also no

Left *Real Triumphs — in miniature. Tiger Cub* (left) *and Terrier side by side.*

Right *The T15 Terrier on show.*

Goliath, was told he had to be able to keep both his heels on the floor while sitting astride the new design.

The lightweight Triumph's debut was in late 1952, and that was the year following the takeover of the Meriden company by the BSA group. The old Coventry Triumph works and most of its tooling for traditional singles had been bombed out in 1940, and after the war with the demand for the WD singles over, Turner at his new Meriden factory had taken the daring step of turning over production entirely to twins, and in 1951 had even axed the smaller 350 twin to concentrate on the highly successful 500s and 650s. But his BSA partners, who in his mind were still very much his rivals, did have one string to their bow which Meriden could not match — the little Bantam 125 cc two-stroke, which would notch up 100,000 sales by 1953.

Turner set out to counter this. The lightweight motorcycle market in Britain was ripe for a breakthrough, with the LE priced beyond the range of most and lacking appeal to young enthusiasts, and the 4.5 bhp D 1 Bantams or two-stroke Villiers-engined stodge practically the only alternatives, though scooters from the Continent were already a growing factor. But Triumph had no experience with two-strokes, Turner did not like them, and they lacked sales appeal in the major market he was developing, the United States.

He further justified the choice of a four-stroke by the fact that it would produce 'the maximum power output for a given capacity' (which was true then but not now), and on the grounds of reliability, a claim that would ring a little hollow shortly afterwards. He felt 150 cc capacity would provide 'ample power for two, at 45/50 mph, with 60 as top speed. That's enough for the majority of motor cyclists', which was also probably true at that time.

With typical Turner panache, it was claimed that in just six and a half weeks this new machine passed from drawing board to experimental prototype stage. One source provides a possible explanation for this incredible speed; that the

basis of the Terrier had been provided by existing drawings of a similar design deriving from Terrot of Dijon. Peugeot, the French Triumph importers, had also taken over Terrot, and were then said to have supplied the blueprints to Turner. Even the Terrot/Terrier names are suggestive, but we shall probably never know, since as his draughtsman Jack Wickes put it, 'Edward Turner would rather die than be seen to copy'. Whatever the truth, the new design set the trend in British lightweights for the next two decades.

The T15 Terrier was a sensation at the Earls Court show late in 1952. It may not have been the cheapest lightweight but it was very competitively priced at £125, and full of irresistibly modern features. There was unit construction of the engine and gearbox, and with four speeds in the box when the Bantam and most Villiers engines only boasted three. The basic engine design was innovative. Almost all British engines had their crankcase castings split along the centre line and were then built up around the crankshaft. By contrast the Terrier's case was split to the left of the centre line, and once the crankshaft had been fed into the main casting from that side, a 'door' casting was fitted to complete the arrangement, with the 'door' also carrying the drive side main bearing. This arrangement made for ease of maintenance, but would be found to contain a serious flaw.

At a time when rigid machines were still much marketed, the Terrier featured full suspension front and rear; the latter was provided by the only plunger system Triumph would ever offer, until the swinging-arm frame came for the Cub for 1957. There was also ignition and lighting by alternator and coil, a newfangled system available to manufacturers since 1950, which Turner was backing by fitting to his roadster 500 Speed Twin for 1953, displacing the tried and true magneto on grounds of lightness, ease of starting, neatness — and cheaper cost, always a Turner imperative.

But the most instant impact of the tiny Triumph was its appearance. It was finished in Amaranth Red, just like the popular Speed Twin, with the graceful lines of the headlamp nacelle, pullback handlebars and the four-bar styling strip on its shapely tank, all cleverly echoing the big twins; while the inclined cylinder, like that of the Bantam, leaned eagerly forward, matching the lines of the frame downtube, at the same time as keeping height down. Genuinely lightweight at just 175 lb dry, and as low as Turner had wished with a saddle height of 27½ in, this was a real Triumph in minature indeed, and one which as Turner intended, would frequently hook novice riders on Triumph style for the rest of their riding lives.

At that 1952 show, dealer and public response to the Terrier was so enthusiastic that Triumph pushed on with production, as ex-Triumph Service Manager John Nelson put it, 'before some of the basic bugs had been eliminated'. These bugs will be found detailed in the next section, but they included clutch problems, and premature failure of the plain timing side main bearings, and particularly of the Terrier's initial roller big end bearing in the con rod, due according to Nelson to 'manufacturing shortcomings'. Unfortunately this soon led to a change to more characteristically Triumph plain steel-backed white metal big ends, which themselves would prove an ongoing source of problems.

Everyone liked the low weight of a Triumph. It resulted from Turner's designs, which most of his colleagues now admit needed careful vetting, using 'the minimum of metal to do the maximum of work'. But unfortunate side-effects of this philosophy would make themselves felt with the Terrier and Cub's engine, where the unique off-centre crankcase split produced cases insubstantial enough to be prone to flexing under hard use, and consequential problems. Difficulties also arose from the frame's long 'swan neck' steering head and from the practice of using the petrol tank as a (lightly) stressed frame member. As a consequence of the various teething troubles, the new light-weight didn't actually turn up in the showrooms till July/August 1953, with the clutch/big end problems intact.

Flaws could then be easily overlooked, for riders soon found that the good-looking machine had handling and brakes largely unequalled at that time in its class. It was also terrific fun to ride, with the light weight encouraging spirited bend-swinging. The suspension was comfortable too, with either the standard sprung saddle or the optional dual seat; for although these singles were full-sized motorcycles, since most purchasers of new machines were grown men bulked out by the heavy riding gear of the period, the saddle was a bit of a perch, and many opted for the dual seat, which would come standard on the Cub.

Economy, especially miles per gallon, was another big appeal in those still austere days. The 149 cc Terrier also came in for cheap under-150 cc road tax. Late in 1953, Turner and two cohorts, to emphasize the little bike's excellent value and help scotch rumours of unreliability, undertook the 1,000 mile 'Gaffers Gallop' from Lands End to John O'Groats. The mpg returned

A Mike Estall-restored 1954 Terrier engine, internally sleeved down to 125 cc for a learner.

Above *T15 Terrier.*

Left *Johny Giles, Triumph works Trials star, half-on his Tiger Cub.*

was a remarkable 108.61, despite a very respectable average speed of 36.8 mph.

The Terrier was joined for 1954 by the 199 cc Tiger Cub. It evidently hit the spot and would sell 100,000, 10 times the number for the Terrier. Not for the first time; another lightweight favourite, the Vespa scooter, had started out in 1945 at 100 cc and soon been hiked to the more satisfactory 125 cc, which is still with us today.

The 'Tiger' in Tiger Cub in Triumph terms indicated a sports model, something emphasized by the pale Shell Blue Sheen finish which it shared with the sports T100/T110 twins, and by the first Cubs' high-level exhaust. The T20 Cub was really a bored and stroked Terrier with its power output only raised from 8.3 to 10 bhp, but this put top speed even on the cooking version above 65 mph. That was the stuff the lads, and the Americans, wanted, and hang the road tax. After that the Terrier only lasted until the end of 1956.

We see here the start of a contradiction, though not a fatal one, with a sensible economical model, initially billed as 'a safety motorcycle', turning into a tool for Triumph tearaways, as well as for the sports use which Turner discouraged.

Sporting versions don't much concern this volume, but it's worth mentioning that the Cub was soon adapted for Trials. There were some unsuitable features such as the weak frame, the engine running hot enough for its $2^3/_4$ pints of oil to boil and evaporate, and rapid disablement in mud due to inadequate rear mudguard clearance causing the back wheel to clog. But these were offset by agility and an excellent power–weight ratio, and the Cub was quite successful both as an economical Clubman ride and in works hands, culminating in Roy Peplow's epoch-making 1959 Scottish Six-Day Trial victory. In scrambles they were less happy, an 'experts only' ride, due to their over-short, fragile chassis.

Road racing was more popular, spurred on by proof positive of potential in America, when at Bonneville Salt Flats in 1959 a streamlined, dope-burning Cub took that category of AMA record at 139.82 mph. In American Enduro-style events and, in purpose-built frames, on the dirt tracks, the Cub was a popular choice. In the UK by 1963 a Cub-class race category was attempted, but it was the cheaper Bantams which formed the basis of a more successful club. All this meant that tuning goodies like remote float-bowl carburettors, interference valve springs, heavy-duty piston rings, and even US 220 cc barrel conversions, as well as TIB 4, the factory-tuning bible, became available to the go-faster youth in the street. But frequently expertise didn't match enthusiasm, and the Cub could go fast, but usually not for long.

'They had too much performance for their own good,' recalls Mike Estall, today's leading Cub expert, who as a teenager bought a new one in 1956. 'They would burn off any scooter, most lightweights and many larger machines,' but thrashing them had a cost; after three years and 40,000 miles, Mike had run two big ends, two sets of main bearings, broken a valve-guide, seized the engine, and split one crankcase — plus 'many minor ills'. Hard riding could reduce this still further; off-road guru and photographer Don Morley, on the road 'ran every bearing' on his 1960 model between 3,000 and 5,000 miles.

One problem was that the young dudes who were naturally attracted to the Cub's liveliness were also likely to neglect the literally vital maintenance. The minimal oil had to be changed every 1,000 miles, the crankshaft sludge-trap had to be cleaned out on a regular basis, and the swinging arm lubricated. This is one reason Cubs are rather thin on the ground today. They wore out and were discarded. One reason why people put up with their faults was that they were cheap to fix. John Nelson points out that parts and labour for an entire new big end assembly only cost around £6 right to the finish of production; although that presupposes that you could get your engine to a Triumph dealer or to Meriden, so it can't have been that much consolation to some export customers. The home mechanic didn't have it all that easy, either. 'Radco', doyen of vintage restorers, wrote that 'the only time I ever rode a Tiger Cub it ran its big end. I can't say that I enjoyed the rebuild of that little engine with its motley collection of screw-threads.'

The Tiger Cub's popularity was undeniable though, and when not thrashed they could be tough and reliable. The writer Anthony Smith rode a second-hand T20 up Africa from the Cape to Cairo in 1961, and the couple of things that went wrong could be fixed by local mechanics. (He also used the same bike and another for his son to do the reverse trip 20 years later. A great idea, but that journey was less happy. Neither Smith was mechanically minded, they were plagued with breakdowns, and politics plus the collapse of Africa's infrastructure meant that the majority of the journey was done with the bikes loaded on to trucks or trains.)

So Cubs were fun to ride but could be tiresome. As well as ongoing plain big end and main bearing problems, there were troublesome electrics — an alternator wiring harness is more complicated than a magneto's, the mushroom-shaped distributor located behind the cylinder featured vulnerable bushes that could disturb the points gap all too easily, and a wear-prone clamp that could slip and alter the timing. Cubs ran hot, as the oil pump too was minimal and trouble-prone; works Trials men were already fitting larger pumps off the twins.

As the 1950s progressed, efforts to remedy some of these problems were not terribly successful, but the public didn't seem to mind. Annual Cub sales topped 10,000 in 1959 and exceeded that figure until 1962. Turner dealt with the apparent contradiction between utility mount and roadburner by catering for both categories. The basic T20 followed the everyman road for 1956, when it adopted 16 in wheels (Meriden fitters called this model 'chubby Cub') and again in 1959 when it took on partial rear enclosure with the tin 'bikini' panels, by which time its dry weight was hiked up to 215 lb. The same separation was happening with Triumph's twins, with the small-wheeled, 'bathtub'-faired 3TA on one hand and on the other the first roadburning twin carb Bonneville 650s. The Cub equivalents were the many sports models, starting with the 1957 T20C, and progressing to the 1961 S/L, one of several (the first had been in the 1959 T20S) in which a sports cam, 9:1 compression, etc, produced 14.5 bhp and hauled top speed towards 80 mph. In trail, trials, scrambles, Enduro or street scrambler form, with larger wheels and tyres, heavy duty forks off the twins, high-level exhausts, close or wide ratio gearing and separate headlamps, these sports models were the equivalent of the Trophy & Bonneville twins, whose two-tone red or blue and silver colour schemes they echoed. This dual approach made the Cub almost the only lightweight sales success to counter the '50s scooter craze.

*T20 Tiger Cub may
have been enclosed, but
it could still prove an
attraction...*

Sadly these sporting Cubs were all blighted by their use of Lucas' temperamental Energy Transfer electrics, until the Sports roadster S/H model for 1962. The Bantam, by now grown to 175 cc, might be more reliable, but the Tiger Cub was undeniably the one for junior rockers. It was fast, flashy, and noisy, really noticeably so. 'I could not stand the exhaust note of this little

*A Trials Cub doing its
stuff in 1962.*

lightweight', wrote 'Radco', calling it 'the most uninteresting *blat-blat* that ever escaped from a silencer'. Even the notoriously forgiving *Motor Cycle* road-testers at the time disapprovingly noted 'a hard flat exhaust note of consider-able volume', words representing a real smack on the wrist in those days. There were various attempts by Meriden to throttle the bark, and it has been suggested that further power increases for the Cub's engine were inhibited in this way. But the design's fragility was probably a more decisive factor.

Over at BSA, in 1958 had come the C15 single, an apparent rival for the Cub. But if one looked a little closer it became clear that this new unit 250 was actually an adaptation of Triumph's little 200. After a palace revolution at BSA board level, Edward Turner in 1957 had become director of the Automotive Division of the whole BSA group, and he quickly imposed his own design to replace Small Heath's ageing pre-unit 250s, and ultimately their 350 and 500 singles as well.

The new machines, which had upright cylinders, were clearly BSAs, with a more substantial frame and full, fairly weighty cycle parts, in line with Small Heath's rather plodding, middle-of-the-road image; they were substantially heavier than the Cub, at around 280 lb dry. But while undeniably a good seller for BSA, the new unit 250, which was soon joined by the 350 cc B40, also inherited many of the Cub's problems.

BSA, particularly in the shape of Bert Perrigo, gradually both overcame some of those problems for the roadsters, and adapted the unit singles into very effective competition irons. As we shall see in the next chapter, the final versions would actually outlast the Cub by several years.

But back in the '50s, the early C15s lacked the Cub's charisma. And eventu-ally, one by one, the Triumph engine's major problems were addressed. 1960 saw the crankcase castings changed to a conventional centre split (and leak-prone) design, which strengthened the bottom end. For 1961 there was a much-improved oil pump, and for '62 another; and during that model year, a new crankpin assembly which stiffened the big end and replaced the quick-wearing timing-side main bearing with a more robust ball bearing. Apparently this had been developed for the military T20 WD and MWD models, which would be supplied to home and foreign armed forces in some numbers from then on. 1963 also saw the electrics much improved (two years ahead of BSA's similar C15) by the elimination of the distributor, with the points repositioned in the side of the timing case.

From then on the Cubs had real stamina, but sadly they had already peaked for a number of reasons. The home market for motorcycles contracted sharply after 1960 due to affluence and cheap cars. Edward Turner stood down at Meriden after 1963. He might have fought the Cub's corner for a major revamp, but that is far from certain. An overhead cam version was the obvious next step, the one Honda took with their own very successful inclined-cylinder four-stroke single. But the ageing Turner had seen for himself the Japanese technological miracle, and concluded that the British industry could not com-pete in the lightweight class.

On the street in the early 1960s the reliability and equipment level of smaller Japanese models was already becoming known to the Cub's detriment. Mike Estall has a telling statistic: in the five years from 1965, only 10,000 civilian Cubs were sold. Turner's thinking influenced the new generation of BSA/

A Small Heath Tiger, the Super Cub for 1967, last full production year, with cycle parts mostly Bantam.

Triumph management, who concentrated on streamlining production of big bikes for the American market. So that more twins could be built at Meriden, in 1965 they announced the forthcoming shift of Cub production to the BSA factory at Small Heath, where the engine would be put in Bantam cycle parts. While this was an affront to Triumph lovers in and outside of the factory, in view of the declining sales trends it did make some sense. Though some early Small Heath-built engines had to be sent back to Meriden for re-assembly, the 1966-on Bantam Cub/Super Cub, with the final benefit of a needle-roller bearing big end, were not at all bad bikes, a little larger and with handling on a par with their predecessors. But the bulk Cub order in those years was for the military model, 7,000 of which were ordered by the French Army; though Mike Estall's researches to date suggest that only a total of somewhere between 750 and 1,500 were actually produced and delivered. The curtain fell for the civilian Cub during 1968, with a few more produced to fulfil outstanding fleet orders into 1969–70.

Typically Triumph, 'I'll-get-you-there-but-don't-rely-on-it', cheap and cheerful, fast but flash, that was the Cub.

Terrier and Tiger Cub development history

Here is a short, technical description of the Terrier followed by year by year development of it and of the Cub. Although in the author's opinion the Terrier and earlier Cubs don't qualify as 'practical' today, their description is necessary to understand the later models; and also early Cubs can be brought up to later spec.

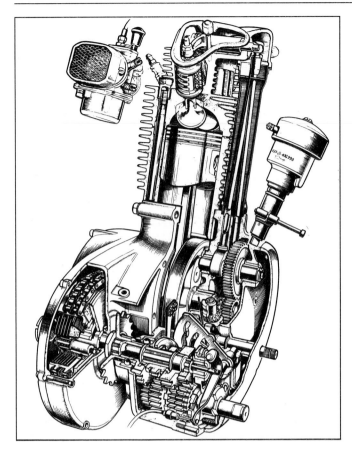

Left *Triumph's little single. This example is Tiger Cub from 1960, the year a centre-split crankcase was adopted.*

Below right *Cub engine lubrication system.*

1952/3

The basic T15 Terrier had a cast iron cylinder, but it was painted silver to marry with the alloy cylinder head. It was deeply spigotted into the crankcase, and inclined forward at 25°. The engine's egg-shaped aluminium crankcase casting and covers extended back to include the gearbox.

As mentioned, the centre crankcase casting was not split conventionally, ie vertically along its centre line, but instead to the left. When the crankshaft had been inserted into it from the left, it was closed off by a second 'door' casting, which itself also carried the drive side main bearing, a ball race; the timing side main bearing was a plain bush. This 'door' then extended back to form the inner chaincase.

The crankshaft was a built-up design, with the stubby timing side mainshaft made integral with its cast iron flywheel, which was then pressed on to the steel crankpin. The drive side flywheel had its longer, more stressed shaft also as a press fit.

The early big end bearings were single row rollers, running in a forged steel connecting rod. The little end had a bush for the gudgeon pin. The rather long piston had two compression and one oil ring. It gave a compression ratio of 7:1. The cylinder barrel in which it ran was spigotted up into the alloy cylinder head.

The head was held down by four long studs which screwed into the crankcase and were fastened at the head end by four sleeve nuts and steel washers. The kidney-shaped rocker box was formed in one piece with the head casting. The valve seats were cast in to the head, and machined to a dovetail to secure them in place.

The rockerbox had spindles fore and aft to take the rockers, with adjusters at their outer ends. They were operated by a pair of pushrods, with hardened end caps at their tops, which ran up the right side of the cylinder; both were enclosed in a single chrome tube which sealed into the underside of the rockerbox. The valve springs were duplex and the valve guides cast iron. Each valve and its rocker operated below a plain dished cover secured by a single lock nut.

The exhaust port was a steel sleeve. The inlet port ended in a flange for the single, tiny, purpose-designed Amal 332 carburettor with its separate float chambers and ¾ in bore, 'an inlet tract you could block with a fruit gum', as one owner put it. The carburettor carried a sprung cold start lever. This was less convenient for the rider than a cable to a lever on the handlebar, but Edward Turner believed in keeping things uncluttered. A tube ran back to an aircleaner within the centre panelling bridging the oil tank and toolbox.

At the bottom end of the pushrods were hardened steel tappets, operated by a camshaft running in bushes. The camshaft carried a gear on its outer end, and this gear was driven by a pinion below it on the end of the crankshaft. The pinion was unconventional, with a male taper which fitted into the end of the mainshaft. There it was positioned by a pin and secured by a bolt. A skew gear was machined inboard of the timing pinion, and this drove a vertical shaft located behind the crankshaft.

The vertical shaft in turn drove both the twin plunger oil pump, and the distributor unit for the electrics. The first function was achieved via an offset pin and a short rod. The oil pump was positioned horizontally in a compartment in the timing chest below the timing gears. The distributor protruded upwards behind the cylinder, and was a large cylindrical housing containing the points

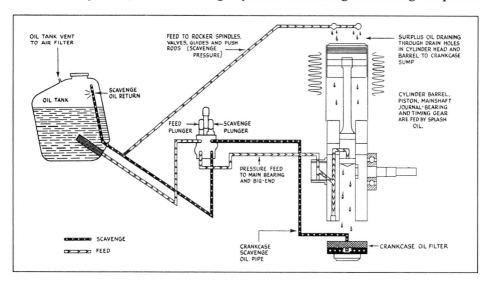

and the advance mechanism. The whole assembly could be loosened off and rotated to set the timing. The 6 volt ignition coil was located beneath the saddle.

The dry sump lubrication system which the oil pump drove began with $2^{1}/_{4}$ pints in the oil tank, which also contained a filter. This was forced by the pump through the timing side plain bush into the crankshaft, with drillways feeding the bush itself, and a further series of holes delivering lubricant to the crankpin. Otherwise the engine's bottom half relied on lubrication by splash, although there was an additional take-off from the oil return line, up to the rockers. There was a second filter in the base of the crankcase where the oil was scavenged from. Engine breathing was via a timed port in the outer camshaft bearing.

The gearbox was located in the main crankcase casting which at the rear was open on the right to take the gear assembly. This four-speed assembly was conventional, with the layshaft below the mainshaft, the clutch and final drive on the left, and the mainshaft concentric with the output sleeve gear. The latter turned on a ball race, everything else on bushes. The inner timing-side cover provided support for the right end of the shafts, with their bushes pressed into it, before extending forward to enclose the timing gears and oil pump. This cover also carried the clutch lever and its pivot, while the kickstart spring was accessibly located outside the cover.

By the time the Terrier reached production, there was a thin rod emerging from the crankcase which was attached at its lower end to the gearbox camplate. The top end connected to a cable which operated one of the little Triumph's thoughtful features aimed at the novice, the gear indicator. This was a dial located on the headlamp nacelle between the light switch and speedometer, and the cable turned a needle on the dial via a rack and pinion mechanism, to show which gear was engaged.

To the left on the other side of the crankcase lay the primary chaincase with the stator of the alternator secured within its outer cover. Three of the prototype bikes had been built with Wipac electrical gear and three with Lucas, but production bikes were all Lucas-equipped. This equipment included a very large ($4^{1}/_{2}$ in) rectifier. The RM13 alternator's rotor was keyed to the end of the crankshaft, and the system's output was "switch-controlled", ie the lighting switch had to be used to bring into the circuit four out of the six stator windings and step up the alternator's output. The system did, however, allow an emergency start switch, an important reassurance to buyers that this unfamiliar system was not completely at the mercy of a flat battery. Behind the rotor and splined to the crankshaft was the sprocket for the skinny $^{3}/_{8}$ x $^{7}/_{32}$ in single strand primary chain, which was non-adjustable. This ran to a three-plate, three-spring clutch, which contained a shock absorber. The clutch had no centre bearing as such, but ran on a cast iron slipper ring; and its plates were driven by tags engaging with the drive sprocket. The pressure plate was lifted by a lever on the right and a pushrod running through the gearbox mainshaft.

This engine gearbox unit was attached to the single-loop frame at three points. The main frame loop had its ends flattened and brought together behind the headstock to form a round section. This was then brazed up into the headstock, a malleable casting, creating a steep 'swan neck' projecting up from the frame loop itself. The near horizontal frame top tube was thus lower

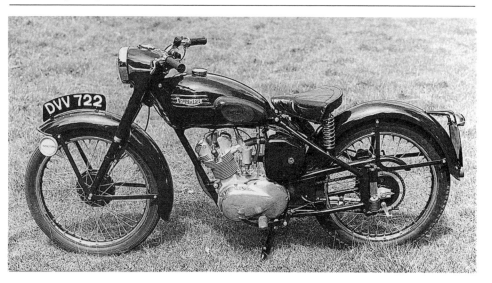

1954 T15, restored in all its Amaranth Red glory.

than usual, which meant that the 2.62 gallon petrol tank sat atop the frame, with a groove on its underside for the cables and wiring but no tank tunnel, giving it more capacity for less bulk. The tank was slung between a mounting at the front on the headstock and at the rear on the seat bracket, thus making it a lightly stressed frame member. It had one tap only. As well as its own four-bar tank badge, the 'proper Triumph' look was emphasized by the fitting of good sized knee grips bearing the marque's logo.

At the back, the plunger suspension ran on rods clamped into the twin tail ends of the rear frame. Light alloy wheel carriers were a sliding fit on these rods, with springs both above and below them; the upper, load springs sat under steel covers, and the lower, rebound ones inside gaiters. The fork ends were bridged by drawbar chain adjusters.

At the other end were telescopic forks which, topped by fork covers and the headlamp nacelle, looked like the ones on the Speed Twin or Thunderbird, but in practice were much lighter weight and had their action damped only by the grease on their internal springs. The single-sided cast-iron hub brake they encompassed was the same $5\frac{1}{2}$ x 1 in dimensions as the rod-operated one at the rear, and both sat in 2.75 x 19 in wheels and tyres. The rear sprocket was bolted on, and a range of alternatives would be available, from the T15's standard 48 tooth to the later TR20 Trials Cub's 58.

The scaled-down nacelle with its $5\frac{1}{2}$ in headlamp carried the large combined lighting/ignition switch, the gear indicator and the 70 mph speedo, and also tidied away the control cables. The uncluttered, pullback bars emerged from it bearing a built in horn button and integral pivot blocks for the clutch and brake levers. Finish was the Speed Twin's Amaranth Red.

Remarks

Hindsight always has 20/20 vision. Today it is quite easy to catalogue the Terrier's weak points and forget what a breakthrough it represented in contrast to the British competition of the day. In 1953, 75 per cent of lightweights were powered by Villiers two-stroke singles, mostly three-speed ones. A crisp four-stroke with four gears was quite a change from those sluggish 'stinkwheels', very few of which were styled in a coherent or attractive way and many of which were rigid-framed. Commuting on the Triumph would have been a lot livelier and marginally more comfortable, and consumption figures were well over 100 mpg. Though the nacelle, the Triumph bars and non-adjustable footrests did constrain the choice of riding position, the Triumph felt surprisingly full size and unrestricted.

Nevertheless, it's undeniable that the Terrier did have some design flaws, and many of them would persist in the Cub. The principal ones at this stage related to the earlier Terrier's roller big end bearing, which as mentioned regularly failed due to 'manufacturing shortcomings'. Secondly there were clutch troubles, as both the drive tags on the corked clutch plates tended to uncurl and fall off, and the clutch centre's cast iron slipper ring to fail. More generally, both the minimal nature and the off-centre design of the crankcases led to flexing and subsequent main bearing failings.

Thin joint faces also meant that Terriers and Cubs would be prone to oil leaks. Three problem areas for leaks were the cylinder base, where the paper gasket provided was not always adequate; the joint between iron barrel and alloy head, where if the steel washers under the head studs were left out at rebuild time, the alloy closed on to the barrel and made subsequent removal without distortion near impossible; and a primary chaincase leak originating from the oil seal behind the clutch.

The oil pump itself wore quickly, a process aided by the crude filtration in the system, and was often not man enough for the job, providing insufficient throughput of lubricant. The skew gear drive to the oil pump and distributor could suffer from oil starvation. Overall the effect was that Terriers and early Cubs, with their minimal 2¼ pint oil capacity and lightly finned iron barrel, ran hot.

The electrics had their own set of problems. Naturally the alternator gap suffered when bearing trouble affected the crankshaft on which the rotor was mounted. The lack of any voltage control in the switch controlled system was not ideal. As to the distributor itself, its shaft bushes were not substantial, and suffered from any lack of lubrication, after which even a little play could disturb the points gap. The distributor clamp too could wear with a similar effect, and wear and backlash in the long drive train to the distributor itself also altered the timing.

On the cycle side, while the brakes were good by the standards of their day, the front forks were spindly, with the top yoke and its pinch bolt under-engineered. The frame's weakest point was the 'swan neck' steering head, and Trials men would soon strengthen this with additional gussets or bracing strips. In the same way the stressed petrol tanks would be vulnerable to splitting, until the factory braced them for 1956. Finally the plunger suspension system, according to Meriden man and Triumph expert Hughie Hancox, was 'troublesome' when it wore, with the wheel moving out of line and chains sometimes even jumping off the sprocket. Finally, the patent gear indicator, as veteran Peter Howdle put it, 'was usually the first thing to go wrong'.

So while the new lightweight was a seductive proposition, in practice it could be troublesome. With sensible driving and proper maintenance, it

Cub 'distributor', the source of much grief.

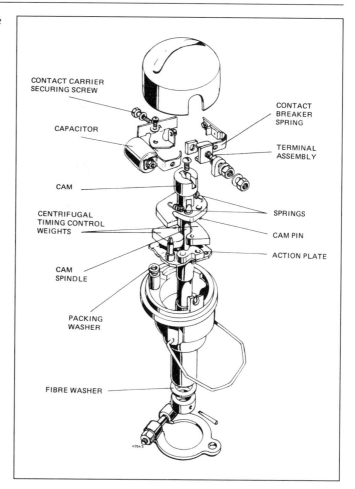

CONTACT CARRIER
SECURING SCREW

CONTACT
BREAKER
SPRING

CAPACITOR

TERMINAL
ASSEMBLY

CAM

CENTRIFUGAL
TIMING CONTROL
WEIGHTS

SPRINGS

CAM PIN

ACTION PLATE

CAM
SPINDLE

PACKING
WASHER

FIBRE WASHER

might, however, reach 20,000 miles without a rebuild, which in those days was considered respectable enough to be Edward Turner's aim.

1954

The T15 Terrier was joined by the T20 Tiger Cub. This ran in near identical cycle parts, but the 149 cc (57 x 58.5 mm) engine had been opened up to 63 x 64 mm to give 199 cc, so there was a new head, barrel, piston and crankshaft. The Cub retained the Terrier's 7:1 compression ratio and cam timing, though gearing was raised by an extra, eighteenth tooth on the gearbox sprocket. External differences indicating a sporty nature began with the high-level exhaust system which was fitted as standard for this year, with the Terrier's low-level system as a Cub option. A dual seat was also standard. The Cub's mudguards were ribbed, and finished with a black centre stripe and white lining to set off the Shell Blue Sheen finish, all as on the T100 and T110. An 80 mph speedo and 3 x 19 in wheels and tyres were further small distinguishing marks. For both T20 and T15 the coil was moved to behind the gearbox, and the big rectifier took over its position under the seat.

Further changes for both were an adjuster added to the clutch centre and a heavier duty clutch cable (at engine No 5360); a forged centre stand (6670); and increased leverage for the clutch (8165). The previous year's troubles were tackled for both T20 and T15. In the clutch centre, the cast iron slipper ring was replaced first, at engine No 8022 by a porous bronze ring, and then soon after at engine No 8259 the same ring was retained but fitted with 16 ball bearings. For the Cub early on at engine No 3905 and for the Terrier in mid-year, the big end was altered from roller to plain bearing, with the crankpin now turning in a plain steel bush with a white metal bore which was pressed into the con rod. At engine No 4859, a very necessary sludge trap was added to the flywheel.

Remarks
Full marks to Meriden for trying, but the new plain bearing was to be far from the end of big end troubles.

1955
With both models in production, changes were minimal. The T15 & T20 had their oil pumps modified with auxiliary balls. Both had adopted snap connectors to the rather complicated lights/ignition switch at engine No 8120 at the end of the previous model year. A smaller ($2^{3}/_{4}$ in diameter) rectifier was fitted, with a higher charging rate achieved by removing the link between terminals 6 and 7 in the PRS 8 switch. The T20 Cub adopted the low-level exhaust system as standard.

1956
Once again there was a determined attempt to tackle some problems. Both the T15 and T20 had an oil pump with an increased output (the first of several

Another beautifully restored 'Baby Bonnie', 1956 T20 Tiger Cub.

and on this occasion the part number remained the same!) and the oil tank capacity increased from 2¼ to 2¾ pints. In the clutch, the friction material was changed from cork inserts to bonded segments. A deeper rear chainguard was fitted, and on both models the petrol tank was braced by a pair of internal struts which ran from the headstock to the seat mounting.

For the T20, however, the petrol tank itself was enlarged to a full 3 gallons. This capacity, though with a change of shape for 1959, would stay with the roadster T20 until the Bantam Cub of 1966; while more sporting models would retain 'narrow' 2.62 gallon tanks. This year's T20 Cub was also sharply distinguished by the adoption of smaller, 3.25 x 16 in wheels, though with the same hubs and brakes. This also entailed alterations to both the frame, to ensure tyre clearance, and to the gearing, so as to maintain the same approximate ratios. This was achieved by the Cub reverting to the Terrier's 17-tooth gearbox sprocket, plus a 36 not 48 tooth clutch sprocket, a 19 not an 18-tooth engine sprocket, and a 54 not 48-tooth rear wheel sprocket.

Also, the T20 was strengthened within the engine. The plain bearings in the big end and in the timing side main had their surfaces changed to a heavier-duty VB3 copper-lead alloy coating. A stiffer big end crankpin was fitted, with the crankpin spigot in the flywheel having its shoulder size increased from ¾ to ¹³/₁₆ in, and the flywheels themselves made heavier. The primary chain size increased, at eng No 17389, to ½ x ³/₁₆ in, so the chaincase had to be slightly altered. All this produced a 10 lb weight increase, taking the Cub up to 205 lb dry. The ignition coil was moved back beneath the seat, where for that year only a plastic sheet was attached to the seat mountings to protect it and the rectifier.

Remarks

This was the T15 Terrier's last year, and the Cub had already conquered the market with 7,802 T20s produced against 918 Terriers; a final 30 of the latter would be built for the overseas market in 1957. The 'chubby' Cub with its 16 in wheels still seemed to adhere to Turner's 'sensible' everyman intentions, but the engine strengthening was a pointer that the little four-stroke was already being pressed into competition by the works, culminating in Ken Heanes taking an ISDT Gold medal at the end of the year on a sleeved-down Cub. Works Trials Cubs would fit larger oil pumps off the twins, for this year's pump modification was not very effective.

On the street, there was really no competition for the Tiger Cub. The lucky young Mike Estall was given a choice of any new British machine up to 250 cc. 'A James or Francis-Barnett two-stroke, an LE, a Brockhouse Indian Brave, an Ariel Colt or a BSA C10 (all side-valves), a C11 or an Enfield Prince? Come on — it had to be a Tiger Cub.' The tool kit may have lacked a plug spanner or a feeler gauge, rear wheels would never be qd, the dual seat might be a bit cramped two up, the valve gear clattery and the exhaust note hard and flat, but looking the way it did, and with a top speed of 67 mph and 56 possible even in third gear, with a realistic 50 to 55 cruising speed, and still returning over 100 mpg, this was definitely the one for the lads.

1957

A major change year for the T20 Tiger Cub, which adopted a new, swinging-arm frame, resulting in another weight increase from 205 to 215 lb dry. In the

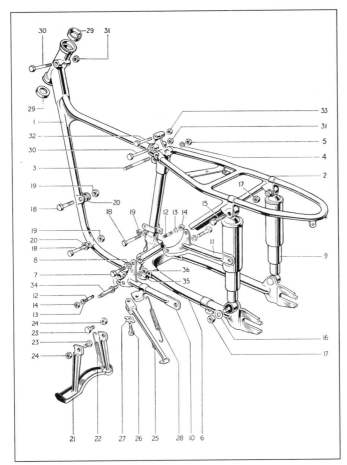

Left *New swinging-arm chassis introduced for Cub in 1956. Note 'swan-neck' steering head.*

Below right *Really handsome 1957 Tiger Cub restored in correct Crystal Grey.*

engine, the primary chain tolerance was made tighter against excessive play, and the chaincase slightly altered to give more room.

The swinging-arm chassis stayed the same as previously at the front, but its loop was modified at the rear with lugs to take the seat tube located behind the engine. This carried the support for the rear fork pivot, with the rear-frame being bolted into place. The swinging-arm fork was bushed, and ran on a hardened steel pin pressed into the frame lug. To match the rear springing provided by the non-adjustable Girling units, the telescopic front forks now incorporated simple hydraulic damping by means of a metering plug. And heat dissipating fins were fitted to the inlet rocker box. To suit the new frame, the dual seat was restyled, with its sides extended to mask the coil and rectifier. The rear brake back plate was now fitted with a torque stay which bolted to the fork leg. The rear chainguard was made deeper and now in two parts. The strength of the wheels was increased by fitting butted spokes not just on the sprocket side as previously, but to both sides. The T20C's oil tank gained a froth tower. And on models fitted with the Amal 332 the carburettor lost its air slide. The swinging-arm T20 was marked by a change of colour to Crystal Grey with black cycle parts.

The T20 for this year was joined by the T20C, the first of over 20 Cub variants, most of them sports machines. This book does not concern itself with pure competition motorcycles, and its emphasis is also on models produced for the home market. But Edward Turner didn't much like pure competition bikes either, so the T20C which was based on the '56 ISDT experience, was a dual-purpose machine which came fully equipped with lights, including the headlamp nacelle.

At the rear, however, the frame cross-member was modified to allow clearance for a 3.50 x 18 in wheel and cover. Also the rear suspension units' bottom mountings were braced with an outrigger plate, which would feature on all sports Cubs from then on. Trials Universal tyres were fitted, though road tyres were an option, together with the old-style rear chainguard which gave plenty of clearance for larger rear sprockets to lower the gearing; as standard, this was done by using a gearbox sprocket with one less tooth. At the front, fork legs with stanchions 1 in longer also featured strengthened yokes, and though the close-fitting painted alloy front mudguard was hardly practical off-road, two wraparound mudguard stays, one amounting to a fork bridge, were added to make up for the loss of the stiffer, ribbed steel guard. A crankcase bash-plate was fitted, the propstand lengthened and the centre stand deleted. Although there was a low-level option the exhaust system was high-level, with the previous exhaust pipe supplemented by a Trophy-style silencer. The petrol tank was the old $2^{5}/_{8}$ gallon one, though again the 3 gallon version was optional. Finish was as the T20.

Remarks

The swinging-arm frame, while no stronger, was just as light and easy to handle, exuberantly if required, as its predecessor. One characteristic deficiency was the provision for lubricating the swinging-arm, an important factor in maintaining good handling, which was supposed to be done every 1,000 miles. But the single grease nipple for this purpose was at first located inaccessibly under the arm's pivot, which encouraged neglect. When the swinging-arm

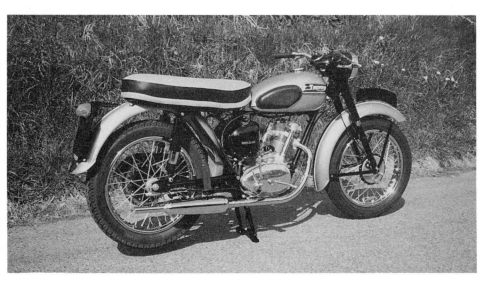

bushes and hardened steel pin wore and needed replacement, they were usually so firmly embedded in the lug that they could not be driven out, so to avoid damaging the frame renewal was (and is) a job for the professional with a hydraulic press, and new bushes had to be line-reamed after fitting. Still, Cubs handled at least as well as their main rival BSA's Bantam, which had adopted its own swinging-arm frame in 1956, and in 1958 went to 175 cc.

1958

For both T20 and T20C, there was a significant strengthening measure. A duplex primary chain of $^3/_8$ x $^7/_{16}$ in dimension was adopted. To take this, the outer primary chaincase was made deeper, and a redesigned chaincase oil seal with a labyrinth rubber seal in a new seal retaining ring was added for oil tightness. At the same time the clutch drum became an iron casting with its sprocket integral (incidentally like that of the new 250 cc BSA C15, itself an expanded Cub engine with an upright cylinder). The drum also featured internal slots to engage the friction plate tongues. To maintain the same approximate gearing, for the T20 sprockets were all once again revised, with the engine sprocket up from 18 to 19 teeth, the clutch from 36 to 48, the gearbox back up from 17 to 18 and the rear sprocket reduced from 54 to 46. The gearbox sprocket also changed in form, due to a change in the oil seal behind it from a felt seal to a garter type, so that the lip — the bit of the sprocket that went into the seal — was increased in size. At the same time the bush that came out of the high gear and went through the sprocket, was now extended into the primary chaincase.

The T20 adopted a new, larger silencer, and a deeper section rear mudguard. In mid-year, at engine No 38130, its larger tank fitted a version of the characteristic 'mouth-organ' tank badges introduced on the rest of the Triumph range the previous year. Most other Cub models would retain the old-style four-bar badges on their smaller tanks.

The T20C now fitted fork gaiters.

Both the T20 and T20C now featured a socket in their headstock for an optional steering head lock. In mid-year, from engine No 39167 both models changed their carburettors from the Amal to 17 mm Zenith instruments. The T20's came with an integral air filter, while the T20C kept its under-tank air box. Both versions lacked a choke or a float tickler.

Export models included the T20J (for Junior), a 5 bhp restricted carb model, and the T20CA, a version of the T20C but with low level exhaust and road tyres, and the 9:1 compression piston.

Remarks

The duplex primary chain was another attack on an area of weakness, as well as Turner bringing the Cub's internals into line for production purposes with BSA's new C15. The revised oil seal behind the gearbox sprocket was an attempt to stem primary chaincase oil leaks, and not fully successful. The new silencer again was only a partial answer to the criticism on noise.

The little Zenith carburettors, developed from a lawnmower instrument, gave even better fuel economy, sometimes up to 120 mpg overall; fuel consumption was a preoccupation after the Suez crisis had led to a temporary reimposition of petrol rationing. But the Zenith, which featured a fixed pilot jet float needle and needle jet, could suffer from poor tickover (there was no

Troublesome Zenith 17MX carb, introduced for 1958 T20.

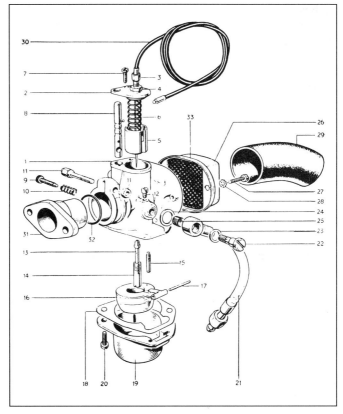

adjustment screw for the pilot mixture) and be difficult to keep in tune; Meriden played safe and in the factory manual advised that all claims should be made direct to Zenith.

Many, like classic journalist Peter Watson, quickly resubstituted an Amal, though today Mike Estall says he has found no problem with the Zenith, despite the fact that with its fixed components there is less chance of repairing or overhauling a worn unit.

1959

The T20 now appeared with a partially enclosed rear end, something 'sensible' which Edward Turner and his imitators had been pushing on the public since the 1957 3TA 350 Twin, though enclosure was not popular with the young or with American riders. The T20 was spared the full 'bath-tub' fairing as its panelling was in the abbreviated style dubbed 'bikini' when it was finally also phased in for the unit twins in 1962. The T20's version looked similar to the later T90's but was not; and it was fastened to the end of the swinging-arm for rigidity. It consisted of two side panels running from beneath the nose of the seat and from a point behind the rear unit fixings, down to the gearbox, leaving the distributor still exposed. A rear mudguard remained in place. The oil tank and toolbox were moved to the rear, and projected through the panels, with the oil tank's filler neck being relocated for convenience to the top front corner of the tank, and to marry with the look of the panels a new petrol tank was fitted, taller at the back to give a slightly 'humped' appearance, but still holding 3 gallons.

Both the T20 and T20C fitted a barrel with increased finning, more pear-shaped and tapering to a thicker base flange. It also had the holes for its through studs cast into the iron, so that the studs themselves could no longer be seen between the fins. Behind the gearbox sprocket there was now a double seal fitted back to back in place of the previous year's single garter type. The space around the sprocket itself was made larger to allow a sprocket with more teeth to be fitted if required. In a separate move, the amount of oil in the primary chaincase was reduced.

1959 also saw the start for an important new model, the T20S, and though at this point it was primarily for export, we will describe it here. It would be offered in road, Trials or scrambles variations; the Trials version, with appropriate tyres, would retain a standard 7:1 compression ratio, though like the other two would fit heavyweight valve springs and a hot 'R' camshaft; the latter meant different valve timing plus a reduction of valve clearances, and hence quieter running mechanically. The roadster and scrambler would have 9:1 compression, which with a larger Amal 376 carburettor with $^{15}/_{16}$ in bore and the 'R' cam, would lift output to 14.5 bhp, and top speed to 80 mph. Details of the model's heavyweight front forks, frame variations, separate headlamp and energy transfer ignition will be found in the following year.

Remarks

The T20's 'bikini' fairing should not have worked as a piece of styling but it did, surprisingly well, especially the following year with slightly larger wheels and two-tone colours. But riders as usual found the panels awkward to live with; there was, for instance, no drain plug in the oil tank until 1963, and the panels had to be removed for draining. The division between the T20 and the sporting models had fairly begun; and meanwhile the new, interim barrel to help with overheating would benefit them both.

1960

The T20 adopted 3.25 x 17 in wheels, and for that reason the gearbox sprocket dropped to 17 teeth. The size of the Zenith carb was increased to 18 mm. The silencer now fitted a mute, a long fluted cone in the tailpipe. This could also go on the sports models, but usually didn't.

The T20 and the T20S, which had now replaced the T20C in the UK, both fitted a larger inlet tract and inlet valve, as well as cylinder heads modified so that the exhaust port moved round through 7°, giving more clearance between the exhaust pipe and the down tube.

The T20S was clearly a sports model, finished in two-tone Ivory and Azure Blue, with raised American-style handlebars, a high-level exhaust, 3 x 19 in front and 3.50 x 18 in rear wheel and tyre, the narrow tank, and a bash plate. It fitted a semi-circular under-seat toolbox. At the rear, the sub-frame was modified to allow the fitting of a 4 x 18 in tyre if required. At the front it fitted a heavy duty gaitered fork with two-way damping. This was based on the 3TA's, but with shorter stanchions. The mudguard was held by wrap-around stays, this variation being in three pieces with the flat steel centre one running to a higher point on the fork legs than the T20C's and the front and rear stays

The sports direction. This one is a 1961 T20 S/L.

being tubular. At the top of the fork covers were brackets to take a separate headlamp shell, which carried the same 5½ in headlight as the nacelle, but also a push-on light switch and a matching push-on dip switch. A D-shaped speedometer was fitted separately.

The headlamp switch arrangement was possible because, as mentioned, the T20S employed energy transfer ignition which had no battery, the feed from one pair of coils in the alternator going directly to the lights. An alternator, an RM19 (not the T20's RM13) and the distributor were retained, and another pair of alternator coils fed to the ignition system, with precise timing being critical as the contact breaker was designed to open for only a very short interval. Without a battery, and with the headlamp quickly detachable via connectors under the tank, the T20S and its successors were intended for use on or off road.

Another T20S feature was optional close ratio gearing. It all added up to an impressive performance package — top speed just under 80 mph, and mpg still around the 90 mark. Dry weight was 210 lb, while the T20 had peaked at 220 lb.

Quite early in the year came a major change that applied to the T20 and T20S. At engine No 57617, the crankcase castings were altered so that they were now split down the centre line. There was no alteration to the fit of the barrel, but the cylinder studs were shortened a little, which permitted the head to be removed with the engine still in the frame, a very useful facility; previously it had been necessary to remove the front and lower engine mounting bolts so that the unit could be tipped forward. The distributor clamp was revised, with the previous external clamp deleted and the internal clamp secured by a single screw; since this was a timing cover screw as well, from now on there was the risk of moving the distributor and disturbing the timing every time the cover had to come off.

US models continued with the T20J and a few of the T20W for 'Woods', an off-road version of 1961's T20S Trials option.

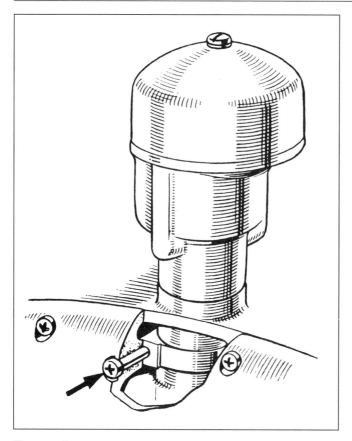

Left Mid-1960,
revised distributor
clamp. More trouble.

Below right Nice
sportster, 1962 T20
S/S.

Remarks

The T20S, taller, livelier, faster and better handling with the larger and stronger front forks, was a very different cup of Castrol to the commuter T20. It was marred by the troublesome ET ignition. The ET's sensitivity amplified the existing electrical problems stemming from backlash in the distributor system, and added one of its own — if set for good starting it would not attain full advance and the motor wouldn't rev out, but if set for full advance, it could then be very difficult to start. A minor niggle was the awkwardness of the headlight mounted dipswitch; and the silencer mute, when fitted to these models, only seemed to make them noisier! Most T20S models went for export, but the ones that did surface here were correctly identified as real roadburners, true baby Bonnies. The penalty of the hot high compression motor was increased fragility and more rapid wear compared with the T20.

The change to a centre line split for the crankcases was a tacit admission that, particularly as power outputs rose, the side-split cases, while ingenious, had been prone to flexing and contributed to main bearing problems and to the fractured crankpins and premature big end failure which had persisted even after the 1956 strengthening in that area. Incidentally, centre split cases should be obtained as a pair, since they were matched and jig-bored together, so the main bearing bosses may be incorrectly aligned if two differently numbered halves are used.

1961

The T20, now in two-tone Black and Silver Sheen, and the T20S and its derivatives, in Ruby Red and Silver, all benefited from an up-rated oil pump. This was brass bodied, and its larger diameter plungers provided a 60 per cent increase in flow, part of which was bled off to lubricate the skew gears to pump and distributor. The new main bearing bush, slotted to allow this bleed-off, should not be used with the earlier, smaller oil pump, as this creates a danger of oil starvation to the big end.

During the year the T20S mutated into the T20S/L and the T20/T. The S/L was another trail-type bike in either scramble or road versions, with engine, cycle parts, high-level exhaust (on the scrambler) lights (on the road variant), close-ratio gears and ET ignition all as on the T20S, though the ignition system featured an additional coil to allow a stop light to be added if necessary. The T20T was a dedicated Trials machine, produced for this year only, and unusual for a Triumph in not fitting lights. It featured cycle parts like the 'S', but a 7:1 compression ratio engine, a standard camshaft and wide ratio gearing. US models included all the above plus the T20J.

Remarks

The uprated oil pump represented a major improvement, and one that could be retrofitted to all previous Cubs.

1962

The T20S/L temporarily became the T20S/S which was like its predecessor but with the high-level exhaust now optional; and with the T20T gone, it could also be fitted with the latter's softer engine if requested.

The T20 began to drop the Zenith carb, on export examples at first, in favour of an Amal Type 32 with an $^{11}/_{16}$ in bore; this process was completed for all T20s by the 1963 model year. The Type 32 was very similar to the Zenith, but its pilot jet and needle jet were screwed into the flange of the float bowl, and the main jet was fitted beneath a brass plug in the bottom of the float

bowl, so unlike the Zenith, they could all be removed and replaced. Mixture and throttle stop adjustment screws were also fitted.

Both the T20 and T20S/S at engine No 84269 had their oil pumps improved yet again, with the same design though a slightly different shape, but now produced in cast iron.

They also fitted a new petrol tap, and a larger tail light with integral reflector. A new square type silicon rectifier was fitted, and at engine No 83717, the T20's alternator changed from the RM13 to the RM18.

Then from Feb 1962 the model designation changed again. The T20S/S was joined by the T20S/H (which probably stood for 'Sports/Home' but possibly for 'Sports/Headlight'), and by two purpose-built variants, the TS20 Scrambler and the TR20 Trials bike, which had short seats, frames modified with a bend in the right hand seat stay to allow an exhaust pipe to run inside it, and ET ignition.

The T20S/H was a pure sports roadster, with the ET ignition system replaced by a battery and coil ignition, and the ignition and light switches fitted under the left side of the seat. The headlamp shell remained separate, but now carried a single dipswitch. Road tyres were fitted, with a ribbed one at the front; gearing was close ratio and the exhaust was low level. It had the 1959 'humped' tank with 3 gallon capacity, and the mouth-organ badges.

From that point, at engine No 84269, the engines of the T20, T20S/H, and all other models fitted a substantially revised flywheel assembly. This replaced the vulnerable timing side plain bearing with a ball journal bearing, with the new big end stiffened again and the oilways altered. For the big end there was a new, two-part crankpin with a hardened bearing ring pressed on to a plain shaft, and the working diameter increased. The crankshaft timing side was modified with a shaft pressed into the flywheel to replace the integral stub. This shaft extended through both skew and timing gears, which were now separate items and retained by an end nut. Oil from the pump was now fed into the hollow timing shaft via drillings in the crankcase casting to a point just outboard of the main bearing. The case was machined to allow a small running clearance to the mainshaft, so the oil was encouraged into the shaft, whence it went via further drillways to the bearing's surface.

According to John Nelson, these much strengthened engines had first evolved in the development of another new Cub, the T20WD military model, which from then on sold in limited numbers to the British forces but more successfully to foreign armies. The WD had sports bike cycle parts, and ET ignition, but with a low level exhaust, a centre stand and pannier frames. It fitted the 'soft' engine and standard gearing.

US models this year also included the T20S/C and T20S/R. The S/C was a sports model with Trials tyres, high-level exhaust, standard gearing (which became wide ratio for 1964–5), and high compression engine, while the S/R was similar but with road tyres, the low-level exhaust and extra-close ratio gearing.

Remarks

The revised engine with ball-bearing timing side was a great step forward in reliability. The T20S/H was the hot roadster which cadet rockers had been waiting for, 'Britain's swiftest production 200'. The only minor problem with its coil

Cooking model T20 in 1962, the last year of distributor electrics.

ignition was that with the underseat ignition switch it was too easy to fumble through 'Ign' to the emergency start position, which if kept on for long did the alternator coils no good. But it was much easier to start than the ET bikes, and accelerated really well to 60, at which speed it could cruise comfortably.

All the above models now ran on until the end of 1965. With the home market slump, production had dropped from 11,399 in 1961 to 6,425 in 1962, and the T20WD and its successor would make up an increasing part of Cub sales from now on.

1963

For the T20, T20S/H and all other models, a major improvement came with the end of the distributor and the points moving to a new position, beneath a

Most sought-after model, 1961 TR20 Trials Cub.

Left *1963 sports roadster T20 S/H, now improved with side points.*

Below *Detail improvement for 1964 Sports Cub S/H.*

chromed cover in the side of the timing case, with the timing side crankcase modified to suit. The points cam was now driven, via its advance mechanism, off the end of the camshaft, removing at one stroke most sources of backlash in the drive.

The new timing cover also now had a hole behind the kickstart, covered with a rubber bung. This allowed the clutch cable end inside the case to be changed without the chore of removing the cover, kickstart and gearchange pedal.

All models were now fitted with finned rocker covers. An oil tank drain plug was added, mainly to benefit the panelled T20. The Lucas rectifier became a small (1½ in), enclosed, silicon type, Lucas No 49072. The T20 finally lost the nacelle-mounted gear indicator; instead there was now an indicator needle down on the gearbox. The T20's big combined ignition/light switch also separated into twin switches. The colour scheme changed to Flame and Silver Sheen, with the oil tank and tool box accentuated, from now on by being painted the tank top colour, Flame in this case.

The T20S/H had always had the option of a rev-counter, but where this had previously meant a special timing-side outer cover, its drive now came out of the previous distributor housing from the oil pump drive shaft. If it was fitted, a matching circular speedometer had to replace the sports model's standard D-shaped one.

Remarks

Ignition problems are the most irritating of all on motorcycles. With the new points set-up, although it came a little bit late, Cubs became truly practical.

1964

For the T20, T20S/H, and all models the engine was further strengthened by the crankpin becoming a one-piece item. Also, the oil pump skew drive gears were now made in Hidurax aluminium bronze for increased wear resistance, and the clutch shock absorber rubbers were reshaped. The three screws in the clutch, which had previously had their heads flush with the pressure plate, now had to project about ³/₈ in above it.

The T20 and T20S/H, both now finished in Hi-Fi Scarlet and Silver Sheen, fitted a combined horn and dipswitch on their handlebars, which also now had bolt-on handlebar levers in place of the previous fixed pivot-blocks. They deleted the central rib on their rear mudguards. The T20S/H also acquired an extended rear chainguard which shielded both the top and bottom runs of the chain.

US models this year included a newcomer, the T20S/M Mountain Cub, a trail bike with the sports cycle parts, Trials tyres, wide-ratio gearing, ET ignition and the 7:1 compression engine but with the sports cam. This model would crop up in modified form for UK riders, when in 1967, after the US Army cancelled a large order for them, the big Surrey dealers Comerfords bought the bikes and hired off-road star Gordon Farley to adapt them specifically for Trials. This he did, and with the help of the new battery-less 12 volt capacitor ignition system, prolonged the Tiger Cubs' off-road successes for a while.

1965
The T20 and T20S/H had the gear pointer down on the box deleted. The T20S/H and all the models with the heavier forks, fitted new sliders and now fitted the springs outside the stanchions; as on that year's unit 350 and 500 twins from which they derived, the spindle lug was now formed integrally with the slider, not brazed on to it. The T20S/H also fitted a longer kickstart pedal which was still the folding type, but cranked to clear the silencer better, and was splined on rather than fixed by a cotter-pin as previously. For all models there was a change in the facing of the big end to sintered material.

Remarks
As John Nelson put it, 'disaster struck', as the new big end material 'just fragmented the world over'. This must have motivated next year's major change.

1966
Cub production had moved to Small Heath during 1965. Almost all the sports models ceased production save for small batches to fulfil outstanding orders, the exceptions being the T20S/H, which stopped in mid-year, and the T20S/M Mountain Cub which apparently only continued for the rest of the year, though examples would continue to leave the factory until mid-1970. Otherwise the panelled T20 was replaced by the Bantam Cub, finished in Nutley Blue and White, which put the Cub engine in D7 Bantam cycle parts. With the 'soft' 7:1 compression ratio engine, standard gearing and camshaft, the same brakes and front forks which shared components with the T20's 'light' ones, this was very much the heir of the previous panelled machine. The D7 Frame, still a single loop one, simply had its mounting points modified from the Bantam's pair of bolts at each end to the Cub's three mounting lugs. Wheels were now 18 in front and rear. The petrol tank was the 2 gallon Bantam D7 one, with Triumph 'mouth-organ' badges and knee grips. The oil tank was restyled to marry with the BSA centre panels and tool box; more practically, its capacity was increased to 4 pints. The seat was the Bantam one with its centre strap and the headlamp an elongated chromed shell bearing the

speedometer and Triumph-type Lucas twin switches rather than the Bantam's Wipac items. Dry weight was 218 lb.

That year's Bantam Cub, T20S/H and T20S/M had their engines improved by three major changes. The cylinder barrel and head became a 'square-finned' type which provided significantly better cooling. Secondly, and probably in view of the previous year's disasters, the troublesome plain big end bearing became a trouble-free roller bearing, and the oil pump drive was altered. The pump was in the same place and still driven by the vertical shaft, but the lower end of the shaft was machined with an offset pin, which connected to the pump plungers with a sliding block; this was as on the Triumph twins, and it meant that although the pumps' dimensions remained the same, their stroke was longer. The driving peg on the end of the oil pump drive shaft was longer on the slider block mechanism than on the earlier toggle pin connecting rod drive. All three improvements could be retro-fitted to existing Cubs, the head and barrel being a straight swap, though the oil pump drive modification required some machining.

Remarks

The 1966 engine improvements really brought the Cub up to the standard it had always deserved to be, though sadly a bit late in its career. But while the idea of a BSA-Triumph hybrid might make production sense, it ignored the very real factor of marque loyalty — if you favoured a BSA you wanted a Bantam, or if you were a Triumph man you wanted a Tiger Cub, not a half-and-half whose looks lacked the Triumph touch. In practice the Bantam and Super Cubs, though feeling 'a bit bigger' (with a 51½ in against a 49 in wheel base), according to journalist Bob Currie, handled at least as well as their predecessors. Certainly in my experience the swinging-arm cub and Bantam roadholding and steering are on a par; and Hughie Hancox has confirmed that Cubs with roller bearing big ends can do over 45,000 miles with no trouble.

But these machines were not a success. Mike Estall has had trouble compiling production figures for the Cub's BSA years due to the change in the

Left *Side points for dedicated Trials iron, TR20 Trials Cub, from 1963.*

Right *The last 'real' T20 for 1965.*

Below *1966 Bantam Cub with BSA cycle parts.*

numbering system and the anomalies produced by an increasingly chaotic situation at Small Heath, but he makes it around 10,700 altogether — and at least 800 of that figure were accounted for by an order for the French Army for MWD Cubs from 1967 on.

1967

Though some production of the Bantam Cub carried on, it was superseded by the Super Cub which used the cycle parts off the D10 Bantam that had been introduced in four versions for 1966. Though the Super Cub didn't involve the Bantam name it actually looked more Bantamesque, sporting the D10 Sports 1.9 gallon kidney-like chrome tank with its chrome styling strips and the old four-bar Triumph badge, as well as full-width wheel hubs. Mudguard stays were now D10 Sports, the same wraparound type and position as on early sports Tiger Cubs. Finish was in Bushfire Red.

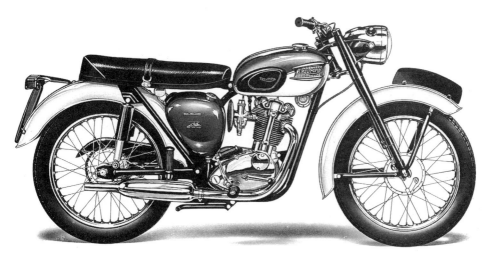

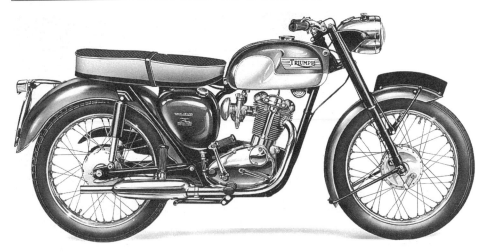

Of US and other models, the T20S/M Mountain Cub ceased in mid-year, but the similar T20M which had begun during 1966 would carry on in small quantities right into 1970. The bulk French Army order was for the T20MWD, and spread from this year to 1969. The machines resembled the T20WD but with the 1966 engine improvements, and they also fitted wider ($\frac{1}{2}$ x $\frac{5}{16}$ in) rear chains and sprockets, and ET ignition. Their engines appear occasionally to have been stamped with 'MWD' numbers, but also sometimes with 'T20WD', 'T20B' or 'T20M####F'.

1968/1969
Limited small batch production of the Bantam Cub, Super Cub, T20MWD and T20M ran on with no changes, though the T20S/M ceased in mid-1968, and the Super Cub had ended from the British public's point of view at the finish of 1968, its place nominally taken by the TR25W, the badge-engineered Triumph version of BSA's B25.

1970
This was the final production year of the T20M.

Tiger Cubs today

As will be clear from the above, in the author's opinion, by the final version the Tiger Cub would make a thoroughly practical ride for today, but with one proviso; if your travel regularly involves motorways, the little Triumph is not best suited. Nor, truly, are any of the lightweights in this volume, but at least with a BSA B40 or B25 you're in with a chance.

I think the '63-on side-points models are the ones to go for, but marque expert Mike Estall believes that even 'the Terrier was identical to the early Cub in all matters except capacity and any use to which an early Cub would be put could be almost as well handled by a Terrier', though he agreed that no Cub had 'the speed, acceleration or brakes to keep their place in modern traffic' on motorways or long distance main roads, but 'around town or country lanes they are well suited'.

Left Last of the line
for the UK, 1967 T20
S/C Super Cub.
Bantam tank topped
D10 Bantam chassis.

Right Mike Estall
looks justly proud of
this restored and
sleeved-down 1954
Terrier — definitely not
a dog.

However, Terriers and plunger Cubs are thin on the ground, and carry an additional penalty to marginal performance — price. For rarity value, a fully restored Terrier is up there with the sports S/H model in price, above £2,000, and our limit is around £750 to £800. In that range Mike Estall at the time of writing (late 1992) believes that £200 to £350 will get you a basket case or non-runner (don't do it, say I), £300 to £500 a rough but running T20, and after that according to condition and originality, the basic T20 runs from £600 to £900, with really nice fully sorted examples vaulting into the £1,200 to £1,500 bracket. The sports models, especially the dedicated Trials ones and particularly the rare TR20, are much in demand and are priced accordingly, though you might strike lucky with a sports variant reimported from America.

This highlights a Cub paradox, that though you don't see nearly as many around as you do Bantams, they are around and sought after. In recent years many have been converted for pre-'65 Trials use; and during the course of writing this I ran across three guys (two of them Japanese motorcycle dealers, curiously enough), who own more than a dozen Cubs apiece. Once the bug bites you're evidently hooked, and the little bikes' looks and style must be a large factor in this. Whether you're an actual Triumph twin owner — and a large majority of classic motorcyclists fall into that category — or a 'wannabe', the Tiger Cub will be probably the only lightweight for you.

200 c.c. TRIUMPH SPORTS CUB (T20S/H)

Since VMCC Cub expert Mike Estall opened a register for Cub and Terrier owners, around 600 have got in touch. It's a particularly useful arrangement, as Mike now holds the duplicates of the Science Museum's records on the little Triumphs. So if you have just a frame or only an engine, Mike may be able to put you in touch with the other half of your machine! He can also accurately date all machines, supplying the details of the dispatch date from the factory and of the dealership to which it was delivered, all incorporated in a certificate of authenticity printed on stiff card. This service costs £4 at the time of writing, and for £1 he can supply a 'Datasheet', with colours, changes, numbers, etc, for each year and model.

As indicated in the history section, major improvements to the Cubs' stamina began with the '61/62 oil pump, and soon after the early '62 timing-side ball journal bearing and stronger crankpin; continued with the '63 side-points; rose again with the '64 crankpin; and culminated in the '66 square-finned barrels and roller big end bearing. Personally I would not consider anything before the 1962 engine mods. But for all models, several of these desirable late features can be retro-fitted.

The main ones are the oil pump, with the improved-flow pumps from '61 (brass bodied) or '62 (cast iron, even more preferable) being a straight fit on earlier models, while the increased plunger '66 type does require some machining. And perhaps most essential of all are roller bearing conversions for the big end.

There are at least two of these. Alpha Bearings currently offer the bearings as a loose assembly at £58.85, or (which they recommend) fitted, including a new little-end eye bush, for £74.25; this conversion can be carried out on any

Cub. At Serco, Martyn Adams again offers a needle roller conversion for '62-on larger crankpin Cubs, though apparently it is possible to fit to an earlier rod but this involves some machining. This conversion cost £88.12, and Martyn will also fit it by appointment. Serco also offer square-finned barrels for Cubs — and they are in heat-dissipating alloy. Linered and bored to either the over-size on your bike or to a standard bore, these cost £117.50. If it is standard they will also sell you a standard bore piston for £35, which includes the sometimes troublesome one-piece oil ring replaced by a three-piece Apex item. (Another replacement route for the brittle rings are Cord layered substitutes; see *'Useful Information'* for a supplier.) If you're going for the square barrel, don't worry about the matching cylinder head, as according to Mike Estall any combination of head and barrel will work, the stud centres having remained the same. Naturally you will have to factor the cost of these improvements into your overall budget.

Electrics are another department where great improvements can be made. A 12 volt conversion can be done in the usual way be rewiring the existing alter-nator and adding the necessary bulbs, battery, regulator and Zener diode. This will be necessary for the next step up, electronic ignition. Systems exist for both the side-points machines, and now also for distributor models, which is good news indeed, for like it or not the majority of Cubs have distributors. Both originate from unit BSA single engine specialist OTJ; they currently cost £53.80 and £59.90 respectively. That still leaves pre-'63 T20 models with the combined lights and ignition switch, which is problematic in two ways. It was a complicated item, sprouting some 10 wires plus several link wires within it, and if it developed a fault, could result in a lack of extra current when the lights were on, causing a flat battery. The same complication means that these

Above left Highly desirable 1964 Sports Cub S/H.

Right Mike Estall with another brilliant restoration for a customer. This one is a 1961 T20.

switches are expensive today, and hard to come by. The last time I looked they were available from Mail Spares at £54, though George Prew did offer a replica at a fifth of that price. One other problem area for some reason can be the condensers, for which Cubs can have an appetite, despite the fact they were the same item as were fitted to the 650 twins.

Finally, for machines afflicted with the Energy Transfer system the solution is converting to the 12 volt 2MC capacitor, which once again involves the Zener diode and either a 12 or 6 volt coil, preferably a Japanese one.

Terriers and Tiger Cubs are quite well served for spares, in particular from one of the few really friendly British bike shops, Hamrax in West London. Otherwise the interchangeability with both other Triumphs and with the BSA Bantam and C15 can sometimes be useful; the Cub's gear pedal, for instance, is the same as the C15's. Mike Estall confirms that the front fork off the 1959–67 D7 and D10 Bantams shared their sliders with the T20's forks, but their stanchions were not the same; Bantam stanchions have a longer taper at the top, and were also a little longer overall. The Qualcast-manufactured 5½ in cast iron hubs and brakes on all Cubs were as fitted to all 1959–70 175 cc Bantams, and Mike Estall has used Bantam brake shoes in his Cubs, though he points out that the rear brake plate for the Bantam will not work properly in the Cub frame as the cam pivot point is too high. Also all models had bolt-on rear sprockets, and the 47-tooth Bantam sprocket can be re-drilled to fit, adding to the six optional sprockets, from 46 to 58 teeth, available from Triumph. Incidentally, some find the standard roadsters' 48-tooth rear sprocket provides gearing a little too high, and favour the 50-tooth item.

Running a Cub definitely benefits from regular applications of 'TLC'. Letting the engine warm up in the old-fashioned way before riding it hard is something Cubs appreciate. Good modern rubber, notably Avon's classic Mk II Speedmaster front and SM rear tyres, will let you get the most out of the agile handling and are available at least in appropriate 17, 18 and 19 in sizes. Keeping the swinging-arm lubricated and its end float down to 10 thou also helps. The gearbox is smooth enough when working, but components are not that robust, and slipping out of third is not uncommon. The only cure is to replace the third gear pinion, as the dogs do become considerably rounded off. Also check the selectors to make sure they are not bent; fit a new camplate if there is any play in the camplate tracks; and a new spring behind the camplate. Clutch problems stemming from springs not done up tightly or from slipping linings, manifest themselves not when the bike is running, but in slip as you kickstart it.

Points to remember when working on the bike are the difficulty of fitting the early clutch cables — Mike Estall on the 20 or so rebuilds that he has performed has found it easiest to fit them before the engine goes into the frame! — and you may care to modify your own timing side crankcase cover with an access hole to the cable, as Triumph did for 1963-on machines. If you're rebuilding yourself, the exhaust valves will probably need renewing; and Klinger gasket material for the cylinder base gasket is preferable to the standard paper item. The standard T20's oil-feed pipe to the rockers is minimal, and this can result in an unpleasant squeal from that area; the answer is to substitute the French Army models' larger feed-pipe, available today from specialist Barry Coope. The pushrods can be a tricky fit; and Mike Estall has found that it is best to time the ignition with the cylinder head off to exactly locate t.d.c.

Most riders today will take a marginal drop in mpg in return for smoother running and cleaner carburation. Substituting an Amal Concentric for the original tiny carburettors is the answer, though for 'round barrel' models, fitting this means some work on the inlet flange. Incidentally, while Cubs are relatively unintimidating to work on, rebuilds will be greatly aided by the unusually detailed Haynes workshop manual, as its author Peter Shoemark really seems to know his Cubs. If you are not sticking to strict originality, very nice and useable Cubs for the road can be contrived. Hughie Hancox ran one with an early swinging-arm frame but the later heavy sports forks plus the front wheel, 7 in TLS brake and 1967 speedo off an 500 twin. The late engine, originally from the French Army batch, ran at 7:1 but with the sports 'R' cam and a 376 Amal carburettor, which still returned 100 mpg. The low compression/hot cam combination seems to be a favourite one for mixing long life and liveliness. Another long term owner I talked to had substituted a complete Honda 175 front end with its larger SLS front brake on one of his Cubs, together with modern suspension units of a suitable length at the rear. Mike Estall built himself a runabout from an early '60s frame, a T20B engine featuring the 9:1 piston with its thicker rings, the hot cam and OTJ electronic ignition, Norton 'straight' handlebars, a B25 seat, a chrome headlamp in heavyweight forks and a Honda megaphone silencer. Note the common denominator of heavier forks in place of the T20's spindly Bantam-type items, though in most other respects the cooking T20 is a very pleasant ride.

Cubs can take it, as this 1971 competitor in the Lands End trial proved on his distributor model.

If you are keen on getting one of these pretty bikes as close to original as possible, within reason and your budget, you will probably be a regular at autojumbles. The Lucas 5½ in headlamp seems to have been a size unique to Cubs. As Mike Estall points out, the interchangeability of Cub components means that it's extremely rare today to find one that hasn't had the 'pick 'n' mix' treatment over the years. Mike sometimes filled in gaps by having small batches of hard to find components made up, for instance parts for the gear indicator, and fibreglass side panels. On the subject of colour, original, meticulously matched paints are obtainable from MS Motorcycles (see *'Useful Information'*). If you're going the cheap and cheerful way, though, here are a few approximate modern equivalents. Silver Sheen is close to Rover Silver, Shell Blue Sheen to Peugeot Bleu Clair Metallic (1968–71), Crystal Grey to Talbot Silver Mist Metallic (1969–73), and Ruby Red to British Leyland Damask Red, as found on the mid '70s Marina.

In conclusion, as the lightest and nearly the lowest lightweight this book considers, whether you are Triumph oriented or not the Cub could well be an intelligent choice if you're young, old, slightly built, female or no Hercules. In fact if you are lightweight yourself, the Cub appreciates it; a 16 stone rider is the equivalent of two '50s teenagers.

And Cubs can be practical. A '65 T20 I test-rode had been abused and dropped by a pair of brothers in the '70s, used as a commute from Kent to Central London for a period in the '80s, and at the beginning of the '90s still turned in a respectable if gentle performance, with top speed around 60 and comfortable cruising just under 50 mph. Its brakes were marginal (curious, as the same brakes had always worked well for me on swinging-arm Bantams), but the engine braking excellent — and the Cub was undoubtedly more fun to ride than a Bantam.

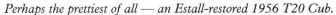

Perhaps the prettiest of all — an Estall-restored 1956 T20 Cub.

On the road, the lack of a QD rear wheel may turn out to be irritating, as may the lack of a second petrol tap. But when you're having fun cracking along, swinging through the bends of a country road, especially on the sports frame with its better ground clearance, and exploring the little bike's limits, or afterwards admiring its looks, niggles like that can be forgotten. Enjoy.

Triumph Tiger Cub T20S/H Sports Cub (1962): Technical Data

Engine		Brakes	
Bore (mm)	63	Diam x width front (in)	$5^2/_5$ x 1
Stroke (mm)	64	Diam x width rear (in)	$5^2/_5$ x 1
Capacity (cc)	199		
Compression ratio	9:1	**Tyres**	
Ignition	Battery/coil	Size front (in)	3.00 x 19
Carburettor	$^{15}/_{16}$ in Amal	Size rear (in)	3.50 x 18

Transmission		Electrical	
Sprockets		Battery	13 ah
Engine	19	Headlamp (diam in)	$5^1/_2$
Clutch	48	Voltage	6
Gearbox	17		
Rear wheel	48 (T20 46)	**Miscellaneous**	
		Fuel Imp (gals)	3
Top gear	7.2	Seat height (in)	30
3rd gear	8.6	Wheelbase (in)	49
2nd gear	13.4	Length (in)	77
1st gear	19.8	Ground clearance (in)	6
		Dry Weight (lb)	223

Chain front Duplex (in)	$^3/_8$ x $^7/_{16}$	
Chain rear (in)	$^1/_2$ x $^3/_{16}$	113 rollers (T20 from engine No 56360, 112 rollers)

Engine and frame numbers

The engine number is stamped on the left-hand crankcase, below the base of the cylinder barrel; or on the top of the front engine mounting lug. The frame number is either on the left-hand side of the gusset around the steering head tube, or on the lower half of the right-hand frame tube. It always begins with 'T'.

To mid-1965, Meriden used one continuous system of numbering for Terriers and Cubs. Remember that model years run from August/September of the previous year, to July/August of the year designated. Engine and frame numbers should and usually did correspond, although Mike Estall has found a few anomalies, ie during 1960 some frame and engine numbers got out of sync, and two batches of 35 machines left the factory with unmatched numbers.

From mid-1965 and the start of the move of production to Small Heath, the picture becomes cloudy. The BSA numbering system was confused and confusing, with the same number being used after different model type prefixes on numerous occasions, and in no sequence. Even prefixes can be confusing, as, for instance, 'S/C', sometimes used to denote 'Super Cub', had already been applied to the 'SC' competition model made from 1962–5. However, Mike Estall has made some sense of the data by painstaking work, and you can apply to him (see *'Useful Information'*) for dating of individual 1966–70 numbers.

Year	Start number	Model prefix						
1954	101	T15	T20					
1955	8518	T15	T20					
1956	17389	T15	T20					
1957	26276	T20	T20C					
1958	35847	T20	T20C	T20J	T20CA			
1959	45312	T20	T20C	T20J	T20CA	T20S		
1960	56360	T20	T20S	T20J	T20W			
1961	69517	T20	T20S	T20J	T20T	T20S/L		
1962	81890	T20	T20S/H	T20S/S	T20SC	T20SR	TS20	TR20
1963	88347	T20	T20S/H	T20SS	T20SC	T20SR	TS20	
						TR20	T20WD	
1964	94600	T20	T20S/H	T20SS	T20SC	T20SR	T20SM	
						TR20	T20WD	
1965	99733 ends 100013	T20	T20S/H	T20SS	T20SC	T20SR TR20	T20SM T20WD	
1966	101	T20 (Bantam Cub)		T205/H	T20SM	T20M		
1967		T20 (Bantam Cub + Super Cub)		T20MWD	T20SM	T20M		
1968		T20 (Bantam Cub + Super Cub)		T20MWD	T20SM	T20M		
1969		T20 (Bantam Cub + Super Cub)		T20MWD	T20M			
1970	ends 10050	T20M						

Triumph Terrier and Tiger Cub: Useful Information

Books
Triumph Singles by Roy Bacon (Niton)
Triumph Tiger Cub Factory Workshop Manual, (from JR Publications, Potterdike House, Lombard Street, Newark, Notts NG4 1XG)
Triumph Tiger Cub and Terrier Owners' Workshop Manual by Pete Shoemark (Haynes)
Classic British Trials Bikes by Don Morley (Osprey) History and practical tips.
A selection of reprinted handbooks and parts catalogues from BMS Books, 1 Featherby Drive, Glen Parva, Leicester LE2 9NZ

Clubs
Triumph Owners' Motor Cycle Club, Mrs E. Page, 101 Great Knightleys, Basildon, Essex SS15 5AN
Terrier and Tiger Cub Register, Mike Estall, 24 Main Road, Edingale, Tamworth, Staffs B79 9HY (see text).

Shops

Hamrax, 328 Ladbroke Grove, London W10 5AD (Tel 081 969 5380).

Barry Coope, 3 Orchard Avenue, Berkhamsted, Herts (Tel 0442 865836). Send SAE for spares list.

Bert Greenwood, 7 Coombs Close, Horndean, Hants PO8 0HE. Reproduction parts etc.

Alpha Bearings, Kingsley Street, Netherton, Nr Dudley, West Midlands (Tel 0384 255151). Roller big ends.

Serco, 2 Bracken Road, Brighouse, West Yorkshire (Tel 0484 715288). Roller big ends, barrels etc (see text).

George Prew, Mill House, Royston Road, Barkway, Royston, Herts SG8 8BX (Tel 0763 84763). Switches, carb spares.

Mail Spares, The Firs, Othery, Somerset TA7 OQS (Tel 0823 69305). Switches.

Smoothline Motorcycle Components, Tyffynon, Crickhowell, Powys NP8 1RU (Tel 0874 730076). Competition/Trials.

Sammy Miller Motorcycles, Gore Road, New Milton, Hampshire BH25 6TF (Tel 0425 616446). Competition/Trials.

OTJ, The Bullyard, Rear of 83 High Street, Edenbridge, Kent TN8 5AN (Tel 0732 865683). Electronic ignition systems and Cords piston rings.

P.D. Electronics, The Old Barn, Woods Lane, Potterspury, Northamptonshire NN12 7PT (Tel 0908 543150). Electronic ignition systems.

Burton Bike Bits, 138 Waterloo Street, Burton on Trent, Staffordshire DE14 2NF (Tel: 0283 34130). Spares and imported Cubs.

John Critchlow, MS Motorcycles, rear of 21 Bayton Road, Exhall, Coventry CV7 9EL (Tel 0203 368038). Paint matches.

Chapter Four

BSA C15, B40, C25/B25 and B25SS/B25T, plus Triumph TR25W and T25SS/T25T

C15, B40, C25/B25, B25SS/B25T, TR25W and T25SS/T25T background

In the 1950s, the BSA Group were by far the largest producers of motor-cycles in Britain, and the BSA company itself, based at Small Heath, Birmingham, had a long tradition of ride-to-work machines in the 250cc category.

The legendary Model B 'Round Tank' of the 1920s, priced under £40 and returning up to 120 mpg, had set the tone. Commencing just before the Second World War, the 'C' series had continued the theme, with the side-valve C10 and ohv C11 and C12. These were worthy but uninspired pre-unit 250s, cheap, reliable enough, but a bit overweight and plodding. They often attract-ed the epithet 'Grey Porridge'.

In the mid-1950s, BSA's fortunes suffered a temporary reverse in the motorcycle market, partly due to a home slump, and partly because their traditional Commonwealth captive markets were being eroded. Dramatic shifts in company politics ousted their Chairman, Sir Bernard Docker, and led to Edward Turner from Triumph, itself a part of the BSA Group, taking over in 1957 as head of the whole BSA Automotive Division.

The strong-willed Turner immediately set about imposing in the motorcycle field for BSA the same necessary medicine, as he saw it, which he had already prescribed at Triumph. Purpose-built competition machinery was discour-aged, side-valves and traditional heavyweight big singles, including the suc-cessful and well-loved Gold Star sportsters, were all but axed. The way was thus cleared for alternator electrics, unit constructions engines and lighter machines all round — models that were tailored for volume production. Part of this process saw the C11 and C12 quickly dropped, the latter at the end of 1958, in favour of a more modern 250 for 1959.

Once again, however, as we have suggested may have been the case with Triumph's own light single and Terrot, Turner's dazzling speed was made pos-sible by some lateral thinking. In this instance there can be no doubt. The writer Norman Vanhouse, then a BSA sales representative as well as one of the A7-mounted trio who had taken the Maudes Trophy for Small Heath in 1952,

*Basis of the unit BSA
singles, the simple
C15, seen here in
1962 guise.*

has stated categorically that 'Edward Turner sent Ernie Webster, then head of
BSA design, to Meriden to collect a set of Tiger Cub drawings'.

So the C15 engine in essence was a bored and stroked Tiger Cub, with an
upright cylinder. The crankcase may have been split on the centre line from
the first, something Cubs only came to in mid-1960, but in most other
respects the engine with its unit gearbox echoed the little Triumph.

The 'Ceefer's' BSA identity was assured, however, because the man in overall
charge of the machine as a whole was 'Mr BSA', Bert Perrigo, a distinguished
pre-war competition ace, and by then both development department chief and
head of the competition department. The late Mr Perrigo was not too impressed
with his basic material; as he once put it to me, 'The C15 was a poor thing, but
eventually we made something of it.' The C15, with its nacelle headlamp, substantial mudguarding and tool boxes, the single-bolt fixing for the petrol tank,
and a full-size, single-loop frame (so much so that the engine had to be offset to
one side within it) looked very much a proper BSA, ie a full-size work horse. At
280 lb dry, it was a substantial step up from the T20 Cub, currently at 215 lb,
but over 30 lb lighter than its C12 pre-unit predecessor (and a world away from
the massive 400 lb B31). It was still light enough, as well as low enough on its 17
in wheels, for most riders and novices to handle comfortably.

Unfortunately the 250's origins at Triumph immediately manifested themselves in two ways. One was the hectic timescale to which the imperious
Turner insisted it should be produced ready for 1959. The other was the

original Cub design, and the several weak points it contained. The two strands rapidly converged. As Norman Vanhouse recalled in *Classic Bike*, 'The time factor was so vital that the normal development programme was completely dispensed with, and not a single prototype was built. The complete drawings were passed straight to the production team, so that the first example of the new design to be started up was a production model!'

The late Bob Currie was the first journalist to try it — and was unfortunate enough promptly to break the kickstart ratchet. It was found that the first batch of kickstart pawls had gone through with the operating edges overhardened and thus too brittle. It stopped the assembly line. Problems generally with the kickstart mechanism arose because, as on the Cub, the flimsy kickstart pawl mated with the internal ratchet teeth cut into the bottom gear layshaft pinion. With the later side-points and C25/B25 models the teeth on both wore quickly, causing the kickstart to jam. If you then carried on kicking vigorously, the end broke off the mainshaft.

Vanhouse considered that built-in flaws of this kind could have been eliminated with proper development time. But as it was, he wrote, 'When the machines came off the track the situation was chaotic, with all members of the experimental department pressed into service on rectification work,' and one of them estimated that about a thousand of the new machines had left the production line before they could be classed as 'runners'.

After these initial hiccups, however, the machine was quite well received. Compared with the C12 it was an obvious step forward. The near-square, semi-high camshaft engine and low weight made it a fairly lively performer even in a soft state of tune. It cruised well at 50–55 mph, and young riders found they could achieve 70 mph and, unlike the Cub, could hold that speed without quickly blowing up the engine. Handling and suspension with the

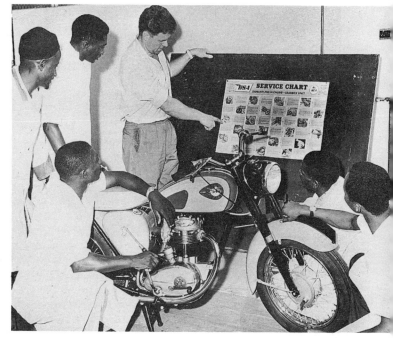

Left *Relations between Triumph's genius Edward Turner (right) and 'Mr BSA' Bert Perrigo were not always this cordial.*

Right *C15s were tougher than their subsequent reputation suggests. Jim Brown of the BSA Service Department instructs trainee mechanics in East Africa.*

bolted-up frame, while not brilliant, were quite adequate for the bike's performance. If the BSA style was homely, at least it was smart. Most importantly, at a little under £180 the 250 was affordable, and cheap to insure and run, with 90 mpg being possible. Finally, contrary to their subsequent reputation, a 1966 *Motor Cycle* Rider's Report on the C15 concluded that if they didn't go wrong when new, they proved very reliable. This would seem to be borne out by the fact that they were purchased by many UK police forces for general purpose beat work, though they were never to be police favourites. Soft-tuned, they would take abuse. Though Vanhouse doubted whether the C15 was as commercially successful as the C11, it was built in substantial quantities. According to the BSAOC, around 46,000 were produced up to 1965.

A good machine to learn on, the Rider's Report concluded, and this was to become particularly relevant in the second full production year, 1960, when a new law confined Britain's learners to machines of 250 cc and under. (The C15 was actually 247 cc, though in an error undetected until the 250's final years, BSA would describe it as 249.) Paradoxically, though a forgiving low performance machine made sense for this function, the new law concentrated teenage dreams on the 250 class and rapidly produced the demand for a sporting version.

1960 also saw the end of the B33 heavyweight 500, and with the B31 350 gone the year before the yawning gap in what had been a popular category was filled for 1961 by a 350 version of the unit single, the B40. This 21 bhp machine, distinguished by the traditionally handsome BSA-style, chrome-sided petrol tank, was in some ways more desirable than the C15, with a combination of modestly increased 75 mph performance and low weight at just 300 lb dry.

But it was not to be a sales success. After a last high in the late 1950s, the

1960s slump in the UK market had really bitten, ride-to-work motorcycles were increasingly a thing of the past and, furthermore, the B40 couldn't be ridden on L-plates. In the States, where 350s were still entry-level motorcycles, Triumph's 3TA twin or the Japanese newcomers were the popular choices. As a 350, there was a direct contrast with the B40's ultra-reliable understressed predecessor, the B31 heavyweight, with its unburstable separate gearbox and (until 1958) its reliable magneto ignition — as against the B40's dodgy gearbox and distributor electrics problems. The result was that only around 8,000 B40s would be built and sold between 1961 and 1965. The SS90 sports version from 1962 was a particular disaster, with only around 1,500 sold in three years.

More successful was the SS80, the hot 250 also introduced in 1961, because it could be used and abused by young learners who would relish its loud exhaust note, a feature of all the breed. Though on either bike, approaching the 80 or 90 mph which the 'SS80' and 'SS90' insinuated was its top speed was a dodgy business. BSA stalwart Owen Wright has written of still 'waking up in the middle of the night in a cold sweat after reliving those experiences in the nether regions of peak revs in top gear' on his 1965 SS90.

Several of the 20bhp SS80s' go-faster features, its hot camshaft, larger carburettor, strengthened valve gear and steel flywheels, derived from BSA's competition experience with the little unit singles. The BSA comp shop was a leader in both Trials and scrambles, and from the start, first under Perrigo and then Brian Martin, had welcomed the arrival of the light single at a time when lightweight two-strokes were turning the tide against the big four-stroke bangers in both fields of endeavour. But there were problems to be overcome. For Trials, these centred on the Lucas Energy Transfer ignition (see p.73–4), plus excess seat height and weight. These applied to the two production batches of the C15T made in 1959 and 1963, though these purpose-built machines, like their C15S scrambler equivalent, are collectors' items today, and out of

Left *C15's bigger brother, the BSA B40 350, seen here for 1962.*

Left *C15's bigger brother, the BSA B40 350, seen here for 1962.*

Right *Scrambles spin-offs from Jeff Smith's works machines (seen here at Padworth in October 1965) benefited all BSA unit singles — eventually.*

our price range. The works Trials irons and many privateers overcame the problems and the C15 was to be a highly successful Trials bike.

Scrambling, increasingly the more popular field, instantly revealed the weakness of the C15's plain big end, which echoed Tiger Cub problems. According to off-road expert Don Morley, this immediately and often led to failure to finish, so Brian Martin rapidly revised the big end, the lubrication system, including an uprated oil pump, and the flywheels, which became steel. Further, by 1961 the 270 lb weight was trimmed by the use of a new all-welded frame, oil-bearing on the works models. The engine size grew from the 350 to 420, 441, and finally the full 499 cc. The latter two capacities would appear in B44 and B50 trail and roadster versions, but the price of these quite desirable models today puts them beyond the scope of this book.

The next weak link to be tackled, especially after the B40 had been pressed into service by Jeff Smith and beaten the 500 thumpers, was the gearbox. Once again, its fragility was such that despite the works bikes having brand new components for each race, they often failed to finish. As noted, the roadsters also suffered reliability problems in this area. The basic trouble was that the compact dimensions of the early unit engines' crankcases, with their ribbed and Star-adorned covers, were just not big enough to take usefully larger shafts or gears. As an interim measure during 1962, the comp shop used their factory contacts to come up with a much stronger stub-tooth set of gearbox internals. In the same way that several benefits of the legendary Gold Star's competition development had been passed on to the '50s road bikes, on the C15F and B40F roadsters for 1965, a revised clutch operating mechanism, and perhaps most welcome of all, side-point electrics replacing the distributor, made their appearance from the competition side.

These developments were nearing the culmination of the BSA men's efforts to 'make something out of' the C15, chipping away at the litany of faults familiar from the Tiger Cub. Details will be found in the development section, but over the years the distributor worm drive had been modified, the plain big end bearing on several models had been replaced with a roller, and the previously untensioned primary chain had acquired an ingenious tensioner. The final major development once again came from the competition department. For the 1966 model year, some C15s adopted the superior C15T-type frame with the welded rear sub-frame; but the real leap forward came in mid-year with the C15G/B40G series engines, which while still modestly tuned, had the stiffer, wider, complete bottom end off the B44 Victor Enduro, itself developed from the works competition mounts, with stronger main bearings, improved lubrication and, at last, room for stronger gears — though the C15G, unlike the subsequent 250s, used up the early-type gears.

In the opinion of most BSA buffs, these were the best unit 250s, but they were a swan-song, and continued only until mid-1967. The decision had already been taken a couple of years previously by Harry Sturgeon, Turner's dynamic successor in the Automotive Chief's chair, to go for an uprated version of the 250 single, producing 25 bhp (hence C25/B25, despite the reality being 24 bhp) — and 100 mph! Because time was always of the essence with Sturgeon, he opted to use the existing moto-cross engine as a basis. What this ignored was that moto-cross bikes were ridden by experts, not learners — and their highly tuned engines were regularly rebuilt, often after every meeting.

However, it was certainly time for a change. By 1966 the delirious decade was getting into full swing, utility was out and leisure toys in, and the C15, despite the improved engine and a chromed tank, was by now looking fatally square (in the street sense), with its nacelle headlamp and sensible mudguards. The new-for-1967 C25 Barracuda seemed promising. There were better brakes, up-to-date 12 volt Zener diode electrics, and nice aggressive styling, albeit it in the American mode (the sculpted and scalloped fibreglass tank and side panels shouldn't have worked, but did). The engine sat in a superior all-welded frame with strengthening gussets, a revised head angle and full engine cradle, plus properly damped forks and adjustable rear suspension. Performance was impressive for a 250 then; top whack, while never 100, was a respectable 86 mph, partly because gearing had been lowered to emphasize acceleration, from an engine which featured the same competition-developed bottom end with its one-piece crankshaft and, finally, stronger stub-toothed gears, topped by a new and eye-catching, square-finned barrel in heat-dissipating alloy. Taller, a bit bigger, and some 30 lb heavier than the C15, this well-finished and comfortable machine was a proper motorbike. In Norman Vanhouse's opinion, the resemblance between the old C15 and the new C25 'was no more than skin deep'.

But the fast new 250 rapidly developed a reputation for unreliability. Main culprit and Achilles' heel was the alloy con rod with its plain shell big end bearings, evidently adopted for production economy, as it was the same design as was found on the unit 500 Triumph Twins. Under pressure of a 9.5:1 or soon 10:1 compression ratio, and a scrambles camshaft with a profile so fierce that it would sometimes break the feet of the tappets, all too often this big end displayed grenade-like properties.

The engine was also susceptible to lack of regular oil changes because of its crude filtration system, and to the otherwise good two-stud alloy oil pump distorting when overtightened. It could even suffer if the bike was ridden in the

Some say this Airfix plastic model kit of a 1964-ish C15 was the only version of the machine that never leaked any oil!

Trying to make a 1962 B40 Star look both respectable and glamorous was uphill work.

Square fins and American styling — the new '67-on version of the unit singles, seen here in 1968 B44 form.

wrong way. That did not only mean being thrashed and over-revved — all too likely, as this was, after all, a free-revving engine with an official peak of 8,250 rpm *and no rev-counter fitted* — but also being used persistently at unsuitably low revs, either by a novice or by someone trying to ride it like an old-fashioned plonking single. An experienced rider was called for to exploit the 250's revvy nature without blowing it up — and experienced riders were what it usually didn't get.

With a big carburettor, downdraught now and sporting a massive main jet, the engine was not always easy to start but always ready to stall, and mpg had fallen dramatically from 90 to around 70 or less, at the same time as the tank had shrunk to 1³/₄ gallons. By 1968 the C25 Barracuda was known in the UK as the B25 Starfire. Officially this was because of the name conflicting with an American car, the Plymouth Barracuda; but the Starfire name had already been in use in the US since C15 days, and an ex-BSA employee told me that in fact the decision to call it the B25 had been taken because the C-series had been so thoroughly discredited by the C25.

The situation was not improved from 1968 when a Triumph version of the 250 was introduced, partly to fill the gap left by the Cub's demise and partly to exploit sections of the US market when BSA machines were in Triumph's shadow. The TR25W Trophy was a street/trail hybrid, quite nicely styled with high-level exhaust and fat rear tyre, with gearing lowered still further, but in the same high state of tune. Its further problem, Triumph personnel and dealers have claimed, was that it was assembled by BSA at Small Heath at a time when rivalry with Triumph had turned bitter, and there were allegations that the Triumph-badged 250s were liable to get the reject engines or sometimes even to be crudely sabotaged, as Meriden Triumph had to pay for the warranty work on them. Nevertheless, around 20,000 of the Triumph versions would be produced.

Harry Sturgeon had originally seen the hot 250 as a stepping-stone. He approved, for instance, of Doug Hele and Bert Hopwood's design at Triumph for a new 250 triple. But with Sturgeon away in 1966 with the illness that would tragically kill him soon afterwards, BSA's new chairman, the confusingly named *Eric* Turner, decided to concentrate on the 350 capacity for North America, which by then had become the company's main market. Since the unsuccessful B40 had been dropped the previous year, the Chairman commissioned the veteran Edward Turner to design an ohc 350 twin. This work eventually had to be taken over by Hele and Hopwood, and as the Bandit/Fury, would just fail to get into production in the crisis year of 1971. Meanwhile, it seems that over 30,000 BSA C25/B25s, in addition to the Triumph versions, were produced from 1967 up till the end of 1971.

The B40, too, experienced a partial resurgence. For 1967 BSA secured an order for 2,000 WDB40s from the MOD to replace their ageing M20 side-valve singles. The WD350s used the all-welded scrambles-type frame, two-way damped front forks, and featured (like the C25 but unlike the previous B40s) a qd rear wheel with a bolt-on sprocket; a fully enclosed rear chaincase; separate headlamp shell containing the speedo; and a fiddly butterfly valve Amal carburettor built to army spec for waterproofing. With the stronger B40GB engines in low compression form and with side point electrics, this was quite a well sorted machine, though as Vanhouse remarks, for BSA 'the order was regarded as a mixed blessing, for the model was by then obsolete from a production point of view'. There was an overseas version, which was also produced in Rough Rider civilian form for agricultural use, like the Bushman Bantam variant. These overseas models had the later Triumph-type lower forks, full width hubs, Concentric carbs, no rear chain enclosure, a separately mounted

Leading the way again, Jeff Smith on the 494 cc works Victor with oil-bearing frame. Roadsters would follow suit.

speedometer, and other detail variations. Over 1,000 were produced, the last 200 being dispatched early in 1970, with a further order never met.

The story of BSA from 1967 on had been one of accelerating disintegration, and this helps explain why the model produced in bulk, the B25, continued with its major flaws intact. Part of the management shake-up under Eric Turner had seen the introduction of executives mainly from the aircraft industry, and the departure, often in frustration, of several BSA stalwarts (Perrigo had partially retired), including Ken Whistance, Bob Fearon and Bill Rawson. These men could have 'made something of' the B25 which already had many desirable features, and really only needed quietly de-tuning (the B25 Fleetstar version with 8:1 compression pointed the way, though cams, valves, carb and gearing could also have done with attention), and the alloy plain bush con rod either strengthening or replacing with a roller bearing version.

Instead, the new management not only pursued performance with no thought of longevity, but imposed a system of 'value engineering' which effectively meant that any change had to be shown to make money. They also withdrew the design elements from the Group's factories to an ivory tower named Umberslade Hall. BSA did peg away at the B25's piston and barrel troubles, its carburation, its oil pump, and even its oil-tightness, as well as replacing the small fibreglass tank with a $3\frac{1}{4}$ gallon steel one, but the only really significant improvement came in 1969 to the brakes and forks — and the design for both the TLS brake and the shuttle-valve forks had originated with Doug Hele at Triumph, who had resisted the move to Umberslade.

Meanwhile, on the shop floor of the demoralized factory standards of manufacture and assembly had declined, and free enterprise flourished. As an example, unit singles' specialists OTJ have pin-pointed how the good facility for strobing up the alternator via the primary chaincase did not always work well in practice, due to excessive machining tolerances. OTJ have also encountered what they believe were reject parts which left the factory unofficially and got on to the market. None of this did any good for the reputation of the 250, or of BSA.

The final act came when the B25, together with a larger version of the single

Left 250 Starfire for 1969, in many ways a fine motorcycle.

Right 1971 oil-in-frame B25T for trail — note smaller front brake.

in B50 500 cc form, were part of the notorious revamped range for 1971. Like both the Triumph and BSA twins, the B25 and T25 now appeared in oil-bearing frames with alloy forks and conical hub brakes, and all-new street scrambler styling, or (very similar) trail versions, all of which had the 250s' weight down to 290 lb again. Most of this was the product of Umberslade Hall, though the chassis derived from the Mk IV moto-cross frame. Some elements could be justifiably criticized — flimsy, fracture-prone wire headlamp and front mudguard mountings, the impractical Dove Grey frame colour (a literally pale imitation of the Rickman's nickel-plated chassis), and the appearance of 'the new speed-styled silencer that tunes in on a deeper, more power-packed engine note', which in reality was an odd-looking black box with perforated chrome heat shields. But the 250 engines, now claiming only 22.5 bhp at 6,200 rpm, (and there was by now provision for a rev counter) had been significantly improved and strengthened, with a stronger con rod, a cartridge oil filter on the return line and an extra plate in the clutch. Despite their pretentious styling and seat height, the new frames actually offered a better road/trail handling compromise than the Japanese machines they were intended to compete with, with the 250 in some ways preferable off-road to the arm-wrenching 500, on which the weight, though only some 20 lb more, seemed further forward and higher up.

It was a pity, therefore, that BSA had reached very nearly the end of the line. Although the oil-in-frame singles in both BSA and Triumph versions continued to be churned out in their thousands past the point that was prudent, for the 250s the chop finally came in late '71/early '72. Some moto-cross B50s were later produced badged as the Triumph TR5MX, but the competition side would pass to Alan Clews' CCM, who kept the thumpers alive off-road for another decade, and is today still a source of engine spares, some strengthened, for the late 250s. Just as well, because although they were undeniably flawed in some ways several versions of the BSA singles were very likeable, and today more than ever it is possible to make something of them. They suffered by comparison both with what had gone before — the ultra-reliable, long-stroke heavyweight singles with their high gearing and heavy flywheels — and

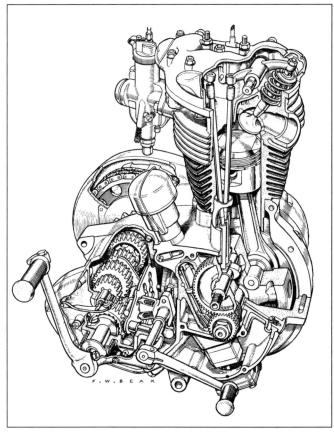

Above *Postscript: CCM moto-crosser developed from BSA unit singles in the '70s.*

Left *Compact C15 engine with four-speed gearbox built in unit.*

what came after, the high-performance Japanese lightweights, ultra-reliable again. But they had their own virtues — they were cheap, light and lively.

C15 and B25 development history

Here is a short, technical description of the model, followed by year-by-year development.

The C15 was introduced in September 1958. (However, it should be noted that with these models, as in the rest of the book, henceforth all dates usually refer to the production year, even though this may have commenced in September of the previous year.)

1958/9

As mentioned, the basic C15 engine layout was very similar to the Triumph Terrier/Tiger Cub; an immediate giveaway was the up-for-up gear change, a Triumph characteristic. The 247 cc (67 x 70 mm) dimensions would remain the same until the end, as would the three engine mounting points, and the 250 shared a common stroke and hence a similar engine height with the later B40 350. So with the exception of the very late (1971/2) 250s, which had a wider rear crankcase lug with the hole positioned about $\frac{1}{2}$ in differently, any 250 or 350 engine would go in any of these models' frames; though fitting an earlier motor into the very late oil-in-frame chassis can be slightly complicated, as there is a frame tube that obstructs the earlier engine's oil pipes.

There were some differences between the BSA engine and that of the Triumph. The C15's upright cylinder was topped with an alloy head which featured a separate rocker box, unlike the Cub's all-in-one head and box. Behind an oval cover on the right side of the rocker box, the top ends of the pushrods could be located to the ball-ended rocker inner arms. Fore and aft of the rocker box were round slotted covers, giving access to the outer ends of the rockers for adjusting the valve gaps, which was done by the traditional screw and locknut method; the slotted covers were a Triumph feature which were to prove just as hard to tighten properly, and as prone to falling off, as they were on Meriden's twins, and would soon be replaced.

The BSA's cast-iron cylinder also differed a little in appearance from that of the Cubs. As well as being upright, the chromed tube running up the timing side was partially shrouded by the head fins halfway up the cylinder. The C15's cylinder was black where the Cub's had been silver. Inside it, the tubular, light-alloy pushrods were 'cross-over'; the outside rod operated the inlet rocker, while the inner one which worked the exhaust was the same length at 186mm. There was a flange mounting for the $\frac{7}{8}$ in Amal Monobloc carburettor.

The cylinder barrel spigoted into the head, and both were held down by four long studs screwed down into the crankcase. Within the head the layout was similar to the Cub — fore-and-aft rocker spindles, and duplex valve springs retained by a collar and split collets, with austenitic iron valve seat inserts cast into the head, and valves running in guides which were pressed in, up to a locating circlip. Despite the upright engine, the head with the rocker box still attached could be removed with the engine in the frame.

At its base, the barrel was deeply spigoted into the compact alloy crankcase,

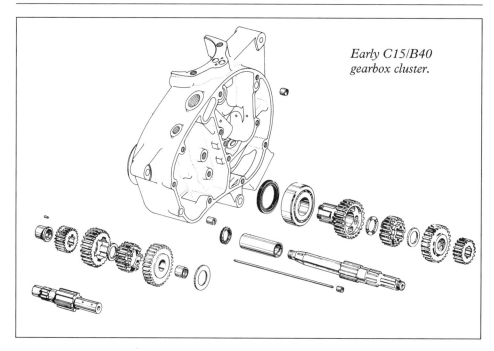

Early C15/B40 gearbox cluster.

which was vertically split along its centre line, another variation from the Cub until 1960. It was quite cleverly arranged, in that the right-hand crankcase casting included the gearbox section. Thus the box and the gearbox final drive sprocket could be worked on without splitting the cases. On Roadster unit singles, gearing was altered by variations in the final drive sprocket, together with later occasional changes for the C25/B25 in the rear sprocket. The left-side

Samson the lion cub with a 1961 C15.

crankcase casting incorporated the inner primary chaincase. A detachable circular cover with its own oil seal to retain oil in the chaincase allowed the gearbox sprocket and main oil seal to be replaced again without splitting the crank case. There was never a change to the engine and clutch sprockets, which were 23T and 52T respectively. The three engine mounting points already mentioned were cast into the right-side case, though the lug under the engine bridged both halves. The engine was markedly offset to the left in the frame which, for that reason, was asymmetrical, in plan. This was necessary because the gearbox sprocket was located close to the engine's centre line, and there had to be offset if the rear chain was to clear the rear tyre.

Within the cases ran a built-up crankshaft with the mainshafts being pressed into the cast-iron flywheels, as was the single diameter crankpin. On this ran a plain big end with a steel-backed, lead-bronze bush; the small end bush was of bronze. The piston carried two compression rings and one scraper ring, and gave a compression ratio of 7.25:1. The right flywheel incorporated a sludge trap. The crankshaft ran on a drive side ball race and on the timing side, a steel-backed Vandervell copper-lead plain bush, with crankshaft end float limited by shims on the drive side between bearing and crank — contrary to the picture in the parts list! This plain bearing fed oil into the mainshaft, lubricating itself and then the big end.

The engine was timed by a pinion on the crankshaft meshing with a gear on the camshaft, which sat directly above the crankshaft and ran on bronze bushes in the crankcase wall and the inner timing cover. As on the Cub, a skew gear on the mainshaft inboard of the timing pinion drove a shaft that ran vertically, though in side view it was inclined. At its bottom end the shaft went to the duplex gear oil pump bolted to a face in the inner timing case casting. The pump was a typical BSA design, and less problem-prone than the Triumph's twin plunger pump. Under the pump there was a sump plate in the base of the casting, incorporating a broad mesh gauze filter. Pressure relief in the dry sump lubrication system was provided by a release valve at the front of the right-hand crankcase, at a point in the system before the oil flowed into the crankshaft.

At its upper end, the vertical shaft drove the ignition cam in the distributor which incorporated an auto-advance mechanism, and was clamped to the right side of the crankcase casting, behind the cylinder — all as on the Cub; though as writer Roy Bacon has pointed out, 'distributor' is not strictly accurate, as the housing and its contents did not provide high-tension distribution, just the low-tension contact points, advance/retard mechanism and condenser for the coil ignition system. The timing could be set by releasing the clamp and rotating the housing.

On the drive side of the engine a Lucas RM13 alternator went on the left end of the crankshaft, with its stator mounted on the outer primary chaincase cover. As with the Cub, the 6 volt system was 'switch-controlled', and lacked a regulator. Inboard of the alternator were the sprockets for the duplex primary chain, which was a step up from the Cub's single strand chain, but at this stage lacked a tensioner. The short-run chain drove the four-spring, four-driving-plate clutch, which embodied a transmission shock absorber in its hub. The clutch was lifted by a lever on the outer side of the inner timing and gearbox cover. The primary drive sprocket was cast integrally with this iron clutch drum.

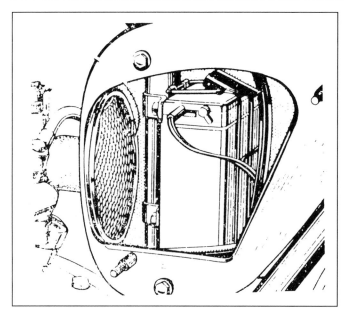

Fiddly aperture for the C15 battery and air cleaner, with an even more fiddly threaded-pillar fastening for the side cover.

Behind the clutch the gearbox, as on the Cub, featured the usual British layout of layshaft below mainshaft, with the latter concentric with the output sleeve gear. All the gears ran on bushes, except the sleeve gear which featured a ball race. Gears were selected by two forks sliding on a single rod, controlled conventionally by a flat quadrant camplate, indexed by a leaf spring which engaged in a series of notches and was moved by a positive-stop mechanism with twin spring-loaded plungers. The kickstarter had a folding pedal, and the ratchet, which was rotated by the kickstart pawl, was incorporated within the layshaft first gear.

The timing side cover had a polished rim and horizontal centre stripe, in the middle of which was set an eight-pointed BSA star badge; both the oval shape of the crankcase as well as the badge and the name itself would be echoed on the new BSA unit twins a couple of years later, though on the other side of the C15 the primary chaincase was fluted in a way that had originated with Triumph's smaller unit twins a couple of years before. The new machine's appearance, however, was generally very BSA, with centre-fastened petrol tank, full-width hubs, valenced mudguards, central panelling for the boxed-in mid-section, and a smaller version of the headlamp nacelle on the twins. The frame was a single-downtube of brazed lug construction, with twin rails under the engine and with a bolted-on rear sub-frame. The swinging-arm pivoted via a pressed-in pin in a substantial lug brazed to the seat tube. The ends of the pressed-in pin were threaded, and the sub-frame stays bolted to them. The sub-frame bolted to the main frame at the seat nose, and the stays ran up to meet the seat loop at the upper mountings for the rear units, which were Girlings but non-adjustable.

At the sharp end, the front forks ran in cup-and-cone ball bearing head races. The telescopic forks had internal springs, which was Triumph rather than BSA practice, covered with long upper stanchions which ran into the nacelle. The latter, with its chrome surround, held a 6 in headlamp, ammeter and light switch. The ignition switch was located on the right side of the centre panelling section under the seat, which contained the carburettor air filter gauze and bridged the oil tank and toolbox cover, which was fastened by tubular bolts. The BSA handlebars had a modest rise, pullback and width, and featured welded-on control pivot blocks. Between the forks, front and rear, sat 3.25 x 17 in diameter wheels with 6 in full-width hub brakes, with the alloy backplates painted black with polished rims and chrome-plated nave plates on the other side.

The $2\frac{1}{2}$ gallon petrol tank was painted Fuchsia Red as standard, with a Turquoise Green option, and carried both plain light grey knee-grips, and the pear-shaped plastic badges, in red, which would not appear on the twins until the following year. The colour was shared by the mid-section tinware, oil tank, etc, as well as the mudguards and their stays, with the rest black. The dual seat was light-coloured grey with a darker grey top and trim.

A compact package on its low wheels, at just 280 lb dry, the C15 was a smart, up-to-date bike by the standards of its day.

Remarks
Mention has already been made of some of the Ceefer's teething troubles, so we'll first consider some virtues. The comparatively short-stroke 15 bhp engine, combined with a light weight, made for a responsive ride with ready acceleration, especially in second and third, and the 250 was an easy starter. The riding position was OK for full-size motorcyclists as well as 'everyperson', with a 30 in seat height, a good compromise. One niggle was that due to the kickstart and shaft being concentric with the layshaft, the kickstart and right footrest were awkwardly close to one another. Compared to separate gearbox machines, the gearbox was a slick item when in good order, with the clutch shock absorber reliable, and the clutch itself working well and cheap to repair when necessary.

The ride was comfortable and the handling, though clearly limited by the bolt-on rear end, was adequate to the bike's performance and ride-to-work intention. The downside of the comfort was that some considered the suspension over-compliant, and further limits were set to the handling by the arrangement of the frame's headstock, where the frame's downtube and top tube came together at the base of the headstock, not both ends, creating a gooseneck which lacked rigidity. Average top speed was around 75 mph with best cruising around 50; and all-round fuel consumption was a creditable 90-ish. Being a BSA, the spares situation was good.

However, the model did embody several basic snags, and only some of them would eventually be engineered out. The first was the plain big end bush which was vulnerable to oil starvation and, as on the Cub, prone to fail. But this was to be uprated to a larger con rod with a roller big end, and as Tony Jones of specialists OTJ has pointed out, almost every surviving early C15's big end has been replaced with a compact Alpha version of this type by now. The plain bush for the timing side main bearing could also fail, and Mike Cazalet of *Motor Cycle Mechanics* wrote of 'barrel wear at an astonishing rate' in the early C15s, as well as brittle piston rings.

The initial launch problems with the kickstart have already been mentioned. In addition, if the cotter pin fixing the $\frac{5}{8}$ in kickstart crank was allowed to run loose, the milled flat for the cotter was damaged.

According to Tony Jones, the gear pedal could soon come loose on the splined shaft, the tell-tale being a dangling pedal. The thin splines on the shaft soon stripped if their clamp was left loose. The cure was fitting a new or exchange gear-change shaft together with a new pedal, and at the same time renewing the gear change quadrant hairpin spring. On these distributor models, the kickstart pawl layout was also prone to wear, meaning replacing the pawl, plunger and spring. The slot for the pawl could soon become worn or elongated, so that the pawl pivoted at an angle, creating wear both of itself and of the ratchet track in layshaft first gear. Replacement was again the answer. Also, if the two flats on the return spring anchor plate were worn, the spring would keep trying to push the plate off the flats, and jam the spindle.

There was also an oil leak particularly associated with this area, the first of several with the C15. This happened along the kickstart spindle where no oil seal was fitted, and the cause was usually a high gearbox oil level, together with wear on the spindle where it ran in the inner timing cover. Then further stubborn leaks were prone to occur at the joint between the crankcase to inner timing cover, and again between the inner and outer timing cover joints, which were gasketless, being sealed by jointing compound alone. All mating surfaces were thin, and even with careful tightening, which not all home mechanics managed, they soon tended to leak, especially at the head and crankcase joints, and particularly around the primary chaincase. In addition to its joints, leaks here occurred from the oil seal behind the clutch if, as happened after a while, the groove was worn in the fourth mainshaft gear bush by the clutch housing seal, or if the seal was disturbed. Oil then seeped out of the clutch housing and showered the rear wheel; the cure was a new bush and seal. The first grommet through which the alternator wire passed was another trouble spot. Oil also tended to seep from the four-pipe oil tank's filler cap, and it was important not to overfill the tank.

Still on lubricant, the oil filtration system was relatively crude, with broad meshes in the sump filter's gauze. Regular oil changes at 1,000 to 1,500 miles were essential, or particles in the lubricant would cause rapid engine wear, especially in the bore and the alloy piston, which featured generous clearances and sometimes problematic rings. Impurities would also foul up the seating of the one-way pressure-release ball-valves in the system, which would lead to yet more oil leaks.

Irritating electrics were next, with the problems inherited direct from the Cub's set-up. The distributor's timing suffered from wear on its drive, mainly on the mainshaft worm gear and its mating gear on the drive shaft. The timing also went off when the clamp holding the 'lollipop' itself wore and let the housing rotate and alter the timing. The early alternator stators' shellac-covered coils sometimes worked loose and failed, and once again the system lacked a regulator so that unless the light switch was used to prevent over-charging the battery would boil in hot weather. Progress could also come to a

sudden halt because on these earlier models the lead from the stator passed in a vulnerable route beneath the top run of the (untensioned) primary chain.

While the little BSA needed few specialist tools to work on it, all was not as easy as it might have been. Removing the cylinder head involved dealing with a couple of awkward cylinder head nuts hidden among the fins. Valve adjusting was by traditional screw and lock nut, but it was an awkward job to perform, as was removal of the battery (a frequent job for topping up, due to the lack of a regulator) from its lair in the central enclosure via a hole in a backplate between the toolbox and oil tank. Getting the toolbox cover back on again, which involved blind marrying of its two tubular bolts on to two threaded pillars, was fiendishly fiddly. The simple engine, like the Cub, involved six different thread forms. The rear wheel, unlike several BSA predecessors, was not qd; and the outer timing cover, plus the exhaust, had to come off to change a clutch cable (though this could be overcome by cutting a suitable hole in the cover to give access to the cable and plugging it with a rubber grommet). On the other side the single cap in the primary chaincase gave access to the drive chain to check the tension. Lack of a primary chain tensioner meant quite rapid wear of the duplex chain, but not as rapid as that on the skimpy $\frac{1}{2}$ x $\frac{5}{16}$ in final drive chain. Finally, when it came time to replace the plain swinging-arm bearings, they had to be reamed to size or the rear suspension would seize up.

The valve train habitually gave off a high-pitched whine, which was harmless and mostly drowned by the raucous bellow of the Ceefer's very robust silencer noise. But while young riders might enjoy that, all would be dismayed by the barely effective 6 in brakes. The light switch was vulnerable to pranksters, the ignition switch awkwardly placed and lacking a key, and the Triumph-style slotted caps on the rocker boxes fell off as frequently as their originators. Other problems encountered in operation were rapid valve guide wear, and wear of the clutch plate tangs, the tongue-like bits that engaged in the clutch drum drive slots. Worn tongues caused jerky clutch action, a rattle in neutral, and rapid wear of the slots in the clutch drum.

Some of these problems were from lack of development, and others came from being built down to the very competitive price of £172 (about £28 more than a T20 Cub, but £24 less than an AMC 'Lightweight' 250). Problems like the lack of space for the stronger gears necessary for hard use didn't affect the cooking roadster C15 whose low state of tune meant that it was relatively understressed, and could settle down to give reliable, everyday service. Cheap and cheerful, the sun shone in the bike boom summer of 1959, and C15 sales got off to a good start.

1960

There was little development in this year when the sales slump began to bite. At engine No 9009 the distributor drive shaft bush was now locked in position by a grub screw, while from engine No 11715, the mainshaft worm gear and its mating gear on the distributor shaft had their form changed, to counter the problem of rapid wear. Lucas 564 stop tail lights were fitted. The pinions for top gear, a 30T/20T pair, were replaced by a 26T/17T pair with a stronger tooth form. The rear chain was reduced slightly from 113 pitches to 112. The green version of the finish altered to the rather pleasant Almond Green. The first batch of C15T and C15S sporting variants were produced.

1961

1961 saw the Triumph-type slotted rocker box caps replaced by hexagon-headed ones which you could properly tighten. The finish of the wheels' brake plates changed from black to Silver Sheen.

But the year's main development was the introduction of the B40, the C15's 350 cc bigger brother, weighing in at 300 lb and bored out over square to 79 mm to give an eventual 343 cc capacity, and despite a modest 7:1 compression ratio, a useful claimed output hike to 21 bhp. To handle the extra power the frame was strengthened with larger diameter tubes, and a welcome measure was the fitting of firmer though still non-adjustable rear units, and of the heavier front forks off the old pre-unit B31 350, with a 7 in front brake in the C15 style, and 18 in wheels (3.25 section front, 3.50 rear).

The B40's engine was externally distinguishable by the way the pushrod tunnel was cast into the fatter barrel, dispensing with the chrome tube. The valve angle was slightly reduced, the small end eye wider and of a bigger diameter, the flywheels heavier, and the clutch featured local thickening of the slots of the cast iron drum to give added rigidity. The 350 also featured a stronger crankcase casting, with stiffening webs and extra metal round the bearing housings. There was an exhaust lifter which the lowly compression made a bit superfluous, as properly timed B40s were not difficult starters; it is best plugged off with a $^5/_{16}$ in bolt.

The 376 Amal Monobloc had increased its choke size over the 250 to $1^1/_{16}$ in, and the petrol tank not only held 3 gallons, but was chrome plated, finished in Royal Red with chrome trim along its top seams, and with new-design round plastic tank badges, later to be found on 175 Bantams, featuring a silver star background with the BSA initials overlaid in red; this was echoed by the silver

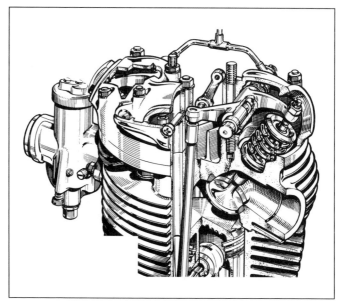

Detail of the B40 head and upper cylinder, indicating the 350's cast-in pushrod tunnel.

star on the timing case cover. Gearing was slightly lower than the C15s, but still meant that though top speed at around 75 mph was not much faster, it could be cruised steadily at 60 mph or more over long distances, and was a more pleasant all-rounder.

Then in April 1961 another model appeared, a sports version of the C15 dubbed the SS80 Sports Star, in a cheeky allusion to one of Brough Superior's genuine pre-war classics. This little raver, a product of demand from the limited-to-250 cc learner market, was the first of a line of hot 250s which eventually swallowed the touring bikes. It looked the part, with a chrome-sided, 3 gallon tank carrying the round badges as on the B40, only with black paint finish, and chromed mudguards technically extra but usually fitted. The fork crown pressing was also chromed and flat plain handlebars with clamped-on controls emphasized purposefulness, even if the continuing presence of the headlamp nacelle wasn't very sporty.

The timing side outer case lacked the star decoration, and was smooth and buffed to a matt finish. This tokened serious changes within. The SS80 produced 20 bhp, achieved by a 10:1 compression ratio (though this was very soon reduced to 8.75:1). It had a 1 in bore carburettor, sportingly profiled cams, and enlarged inlet valve, plus heavy-duty valve springs off the Gold Star, the outer ones having a variable rate. Many of these measures derived from the scrambles experience and, as on the scramblers, to handle the power forged-steel rather than cast iron flywheels plus a caged-roller big end were fitted, together with a stronger con rod and close ratio gears. There was also a most welcome slipper tensioner for the primary chain, a clever idea that sat on the alternator rotor mounting and was less fragile than Triumph equivalents. The alternator was uprated to the Lucas RM18 with 60 watt output. The clutch hub was modified to accommodate equal thickness cush-drive rubbers in place of the alternate thick and thin rubbers used on the standard roadster.

Journalist Bob Currie tested an SS80 and was favourably impressed by almost everything but the noisy exhaust note. At 275 lb dry, it was likeable and fun, though the stopping distance of 33 ft from 30 mph indicated that the same puny brakes had to handle a faster machine with a one-way top speed of 83 mph.

Remarks

The B40 was probably the best all-rounder of the whole series, though at this stage it was still vulnerable in the gearbox department, and the 7 in front brake was no great improvement on the Ceefer's 6 in item, as I once found out to my cost (see p.169). B40s were not, however, a sales success, as both four-stroke singles and the 350 capacity were going out of style.

The highly-tuned SS80 highlighted the unit engine's fragility, though its roller big end, primary chain tensioner and steel flywheels were real steps forward that would work their way on to the other models. As well as the previous big end and timing-side bearing failures which often related to the lubrication system, from now on there were problems for the 'hot' variants involving crank-shaft failure.

1962

This year saw both the C15 and B40 get a remodelled dual seat abutting the tank closer, and with a narrower nose for comfort. Both also had a detachable ignition key. The C15's alternator became the 60 watt RM18. The C15's compression ratio rose slightly to 7.5:1. The points gap changed from 0.012 to 0.015, and the front forks now gave $1/2$ in more movement at 5 in. The B40 adopted the primary chain tensioner. Its 7 in front brake was redesigned with floating action of the shoes to give self-servo effect, but with little improvement in performance. All models had a new-style petrol tank. C15 colour schemes were now red, or black, or Nutley Blue, which came with Ivory petrol tank panels with double lining. The SS80 colours now included a Flamboyant Blue option.

In May, they were joined by a sporting 350, the SS90. '90' indicated the hoped-for top speed, but it only managed 83 mph on a test day with horrible weather. As with the SS80, power had been raised to 24 bhp by the use of sports cams, dual-rate valve springs, a bigger inlet valve, a $1\frac{1}{8}$ in bore Monobloc and a compression rise to 8.75:1. In a close ratio box overall gearing was raised, with a rather high bottom gear necessitating clutch slipping on hill starts. It fitted the roller big end plus a larger con rod and while featuring a chrome-sided 3 gallon tank like the SS80, was distinguished from it by fitting pear-shaped badges rather than the round type. Again, as on the SS80, the timing side cover was plain and buffed. Chrome mudguards were standard and the colour was Flamboyant Red.

Remarks
As mentioned earlier, the SS90 sold even worse than the B40.

1963
There was change only to the colour schemes as BSA retrenched in the home bike sales slump. The C15 was offered in red or Sapphire Blue, and with chrome tank panels as an option for the first time, while the SS90 adopted an

SS80 Sports Star 250 for 1963.

1962 hot B40, the SS90.

optional black and chrome finish. The SS80 tank adopted the pear-shaped badges.

Developments that could and should have been implemented were stymied by the slump. Triumph overcame this with the Cub because of their thriving US export market, and BSA did also have sales there. There was a trail-type machine with the C15 Trials bike frame, and direct lighting, the C15 Pastoral for the Commonwealth from '63 to '65; but US export models like the C15 Starfire Roadster (actually a trail bike with a single seat and direct lighting), Starfire Scrambler and B40 Super Star and Sportsman had larger carburettors, fierce 10:1 compression for the 250, 8.25 for the 350, high bars, smaller gas tanks, fatter rear tyres, separate headlights on the sports model, etc, etc.

1963 also saw the release of the second batch of production competition 250s, though these would be sold off slowly over the next few years. These C15T and C15S models featured most significantly a Victor-type all-welded frame.

Remarks
Ironically, the American styling was not always a hit with the Americans. *Cycle World* tested a B40 SS90 in 1963 and while generally approving, remarked of its chromed guards etc that 'they were less likely to lose their luster [*sic*] after long periods of service (the aesthetics are debatable)'!

1964
There was some progress this year. The C15 finally adopted the roller big end as on the other models, and hence also the appropriate crankshaft assembly and stronger con rod. It also got the primary chain tensioner, and the 3 gallon tank with chrome-plated side panels as standard, and the colour, if red, was now Royal Red; optional finishes were blue and chrome, or plain blue. Compression went up to 8:1.

All 250s and 350s adopted Smith's magnetic speedometers in place of the previous (and more reliable) Chronometric type. The SS80's gearing was lowered by replacing the 17-tooth gearbox sprocket with a 16-tooth version. The chrome mudguards on the SS80 and the SS90 changed to a blade pattern. The B40 optional colour changed from black to Sapphire Blue, and the SS80 was offered in Flamboyant Blue only, with optional chrome guards. The SS90 went back to Flamboyant Red with chrome mudguards.

1965

This was a major change year, introducing the C15F and B40F series. Two years after the Tiger Cub, the BSA unit singles dropped the distributor and adopted points mounted behind a chrome-plated cover in a sealed compartment in the side of the timing case, so it was the end for the ribbed timing side cover and the star motif on that case. The points cam and auto-advance mechanism were driven direct from the camshaft end.

The works scramblers, with Jeff Smith World Champion this year, had pioneered this configuration. The same thing was true of the revised rack and pinion operation for the clutch, which offered a straight line thrust on the clutch rod. The rack was located in a recess in the outer timing cover and meshed with the pinion which was fixed to a shaft protruding from the top of the timing case, with the cable slotting into an integral lever; cables could now be changed without removing the cover.

There was also, at last, a new kickstart mechanism located between the inner and outer timing covers. A quadrant was brazed to the kickstarter spindle on the outer end of which ran a new oil seal, and engaged with a ratchet pinion on the end of the mainshaft, all in the outer compartment of the box.

One US export version of the C15, the West Coast 250 Starfire Roadster for 1961, clearly designed for competition.

Left For 1965 all unit singles got the primary chain tensioner.

Below C15s coming off the line at Small Heath.

Furthermore, the gearbox itself underwent the first of several strengthening measures, and also some designed to give more positive selection. The main-shaft and lay shaft were redesigned, with the lay shaft now running in a needle-roller bearing, rather than the previous bush, in the hollow end of the kickstarter spindle, and fitted with a loose thrust washer at this end. The mainshaft was now supported by ball bearings in the inner timing cover, and this located the shaft more positively when the shaft was lifted. The gearchange spring bolt was replaced by a pivot pin fixed to the inner timing cover rather than the crankcase as previously, so that the gearbox internals

could be fully assembled to the inner timing cover and inserted as a unit. Finally, the box adopted an O-ring type drain/level plug (which can be fitted to earlier models).

Another significant change was a larger bore for the crankpin oilway, in an effort to prolong big end life. O-ring seals were also added to the oil pipe unions beneath the crankcase. On the style front, the SS80's chrome mudguards became standard, and the crack-prone pear-shaped badges for all models got a shaped rubber backing strip.

B40Fs were sold in some numbers to the Home Office and Auxiliary Fire Service for potential Civil Defence work, the bikes being standard apart from dark green paint and pannier racks at the back. Some of these models were crated up and then sold off new in the mid-'70s. My own C-suffix B40 was from that batch. The C15 gained an all-black finish, with optional chrome tank panels.

Remarks

Unit single specialist Tony Jones of OTJ wrote in *Classic Mechanics* that the F models provided 'real improvements for the six-year-old design'. But he did also point out that in the gearbox internals the tooth pinions were of the same size and tooth form as previously, rather than the superior B44 GP competition-developed stub-tooth form; that the drive side of the lay shaft was still supported by a bush; and that the improved kickstart, while more robust, used a lot more components.

1965 in my view marks the earliest of the unit single models that can fairly be called 'practical' today. Although there are now electronic ignition kits for the distributor models, the side points are cheaper and simpler, and the improved clutch, gears and kickstart mechanisms are powerful arguments in its favour.

1966

Progress continued this year, though the major development was not until July. The B40 had been axed, but from the start there was the C15 Sportsman which replaced the SS80. It was similar but finish differed, with a black racing-type seat featuring a 'humpy rump', a separate chromed and elongated headlamp shell, chrome mudguards, and a very silly transfer on its Flamboyant Blue side panels. These panels echoed the blue tank which had chrome, white-lined side panels, but with the chrome in a different shape to the previous oval, now descending to nearly the tank bottom, and cut off in front of the black knee pads. The SS80's close ratio gears were not available, but replacing its flat handlebars were new bars with a more comfortable rearward sweep.

Then in July came the C15G, the C15SG Sportsman (for a very brief period), and a little later the B40G when a large MOD order came in and revived the 350 as the B40GB (WD). The G series featured the bottom end from the bigger Victor scramblers, though the top end remained the same so performance was unaltered. The crankcase itself was stronger, the main bearings on the timing side became heftier ball bearings, not plain, and a roller bearing replaced the ball bearing on the drive side. The lubrication system, so often the cause of grief with the big end, was revised, no longer passing through the timing side bearing into the crankshaft, but now fed via an oil seal in the

1965 C15F Star, much improved.

timing cover into the right-hand end of the crankshaft direct. A larger oil pump similar to the 650's was fitted, and its mounting and drive were altered, the pump going straight on to a flat face in the timing chest with a direct worm drive from the crankshaft. Cams and followers were still lubricated mainly by oil dropping from the rocker box. Rear chain lubrication was now by means of a modified bleed from the primary chaincase.

The gearbox got a major strengthening again, with needle roller bearings now fitted at both ends of the lay shaft, which featured the stronger integral stub-tooth form for the 14T top gear, and corresponding 22T sleeve gear on

Last and best C15, the C15G Sportsman for 1966. Modified chrome on tank is not shown in this artists's impression.

the mainshaft. However, the C15G still did *not* gain the stronger tooth form for the indirect gears, and the B40GB (WD) used the original pattern trials indirect gears off the C15T, modified where necessary to fit the larger shafts, and with the gearing itself lowered.

Finally, some but not all of the G series adopted the late C15T-type all-welded frame which did away with the previous bolted-on rear sub-frame. These would be the most desirable C15s of all.

Remarks
The C15G and B40G at last really tackled the gearbox, lubrication and big end problems that had plagued the series so far, and provided a very strong bottom end, without tuning the engine unduly to stress it. Naturally, BSA only let this one run for a single year, and it is the one which most buffs consider the soundest and most pleasant of the unit 250s. But the company was right. The '60s were in full swing, and the homely C15 had outlived its day.

1967
The versions outlined above ran on to the end of the model year, though the C15 Sportsman had been dropped, the regular C15 adopting its 2.6 gallon petrol tank with the different chrome area. The civilian C15G in fact continued up to June 1967, and production also went on of WD B40s, together with the Rough Rider, an overseas variant for both civilian and military use, both of which we will consider later. But the year's main event was the launch of the radically different C25 250 Barracuda, a strengthened but hotted up engine in a larger, superior frame.

Though the same 247 cc capacity as the C15 and sharing much of the C15G's new bottom end, the C25 was a very different cup of Castrol. For a start, the engine looked quite distinct, with a big new alloy head and Victor Scrambler-type square finned cylinder barrel, alloy too, now, with austenitic

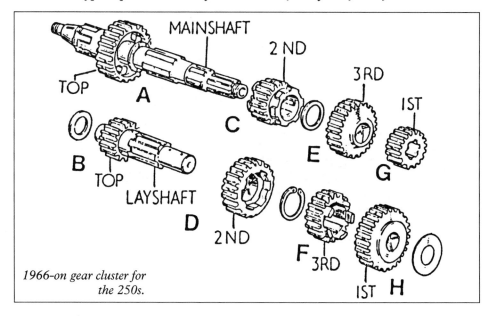

1966-on gear cluster for the 250s.

iron liner, whose much bigger fin area swallowed the C15's previous pushrod tube.

The redesigned head, which featured a valve lifter, had an altered method of tappet adjustment, by eccentric rocker spindles which were simply turned out-wards to adjust the valve clearance, easier to do than the old screw and lock nut system. However, the range of tappet adjustment was only about 0.06 in, so that sometimes a longer pushrod would be needed. That in turn can make it difficult to set up the C25's valve lifter, which was never really necessary to help starting, and once again is best removed and blanked off. The pushrods were now of uneven length, with the outside one which operated the inlet rocker having a standard length of 176.5 mm, and the inner/exhaust one 174.5 mm. The head, with a hemispherical combustion chamber, housed effi-cient valves, the inlet valve being of larger diameter than previously. Valve guides were of Hi-Dural and valve springs were the variable rate type with steel collars featuring the Gold Star type half-round groove collets. The valve seats were of cast iron, but as OTJ's Tony Jones has pointed out, the factory found it difficult to achieve concentricity of the guide bores with the cast-in seats. Consequently, seat cutting or valve grinding reduces the width on one side, and on the other side the valve would be on the aluminium. Also some inlet ports were left part-machined if operators spotted the faulty valve seats, and so have a restricted port. Valve seating problems thus created can sometimes be helped by the use of oversized valves. Finally, the stepped valve guides had a short grip length relative to their diameter and could work loose, particularly if the soft alloy bore had been damaged, perhaps by owner-mechanics banging guides in or out without heating up the head enough.

Further down, the square, close-finned alloy barrel's iron liner was replace-able, which was not the case with its big brother B44. But the iron liners sometimes worked loose when the alloy barrel got hot and expanded, and due to a gap of 0.015 in between the top of the liner and the lower surface of the cylinder head would begin to move up and down with a noisy hammering motion. Piston ring condition remained critical.

Another big change from the C15 was an all-new, one-piece crankshaft with the flywheels pressed on and retained by four radial bolts each, as on the twins. This arrangement required a Triumph twin-type connecting rod in alloy, with a bronze-bushed small end, and a split big end eye lined with replaceable white metal bearings. This made good production sense, as these rods with their same 70 mm stroke were identical to the ones on the smaller C-range Triumph twins, with one exception, an inclined oil hole drilled through the con rod — though Tony Jones believes this is actually superfluous. On the twins the alloy rod worked well enough, but for the new unit singles with their fierce 10:1 compres-sion, they spelt big trouble. More than a few snapped clean in two.

The new crank ran on the previous bearings but in this case there was a potential flaw. The timing side bearing housing had a stiffening web or ring behind it, which was rather thin at one point, and a crack could develop there. In addition, on the timing side end of the crankshaft, there was a spigot which gave a mounting for the oil seal essential to maintain oil pressure in the end-fed crank. Tony Jones points out that the spigot was soft, and if hammered too much to release the crank from its timing-side bearing, the end will mushroom and severely reduce the oil pressure by damaging the oil seal.

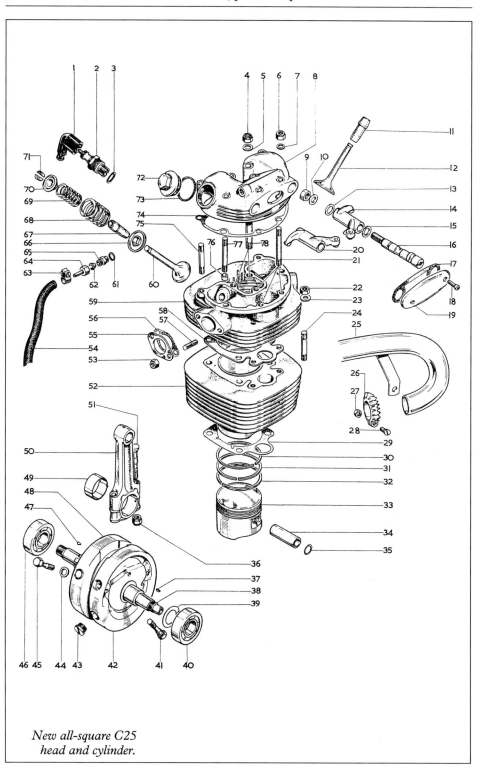

*New all-square C25
head and cylinder.*

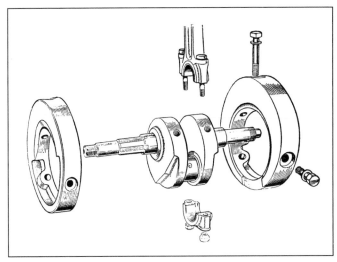

Left *The heart of the problem. C25/B25's one-piece forged crankshaft, necessitating steel-backed plain big end shells.*

Below right *New all-singing all-dancing C25 Barracuda for 1967.*

The new model's timing was quite radical with 299° of opening on that larger inlet valve, and though the exhaust valve was unchanged in head diameter its opening time was also extended. This was combined with a fierce scrambles-bred camshaft profile which stayed until the end, and which some claimed broke the feet off the tappets; the first tappets' Stellite-tipped flat feet could certainly flex, and they would be enlarged for the following year. There was also a much larger downdraught-mounted carburettor, which was very easy to flood, making starting difficult. It was Amal's new Concentric in 928 form with a pancake air filter, and a massive 220 main jet was used in these early models. The factory tried many variants from then on, reducing it to 170 the following year, and the same for the first TR25W, but going back to 200 for the 1969–70 Triumph-badged models, while a factory bulletin put it at 180 for the BSA 250 in 1969, and the oil-in-frame B25 rose again to 190. In combination with their short clutch take up, this meant that the 250 unit singles were always easy to stall, and thirstier than their predecessors at around 75 mpg or less.

In addition, in the interests of acceleration, which was what concerned the American market, gearing was lowered in all four gears — the C25's top was 6.29:1 against the C15's 5.98:1, though top speed on test was 86 mph, and the tester found the Barracuda over-geared if anything, with a drop in acceleration when changing into top. The gears themselves finally got the stronger stub-tooth form developed in competition, for the indirect gears. In addition, the kickstarter quadrant shaft and outer cover bush were soon to be strengthened by having their diameter increased from the C15's ⅝ in to ¾ in, though it retained the potentially vulnerable cotter end fixing. The strengthening was all good, but riders found that the gearbox still jumped out of third once wear had begun due to insufficient engagement. In addition, as had been the case with all the '65-on sidepoints models, the teeth on the kickstart quadrant and on the pinion it meshed with wore quickly, causing the kickstart to jam. After that, persistent vigorous kicking could break the end of the main shaft. However, the shaft would still be supported by its bearings, and you could continue to ride normally after bump-starting the plot!

The heart of the lubrication system was improved over the earlier C15, with the adoption of an alloy-bodied oil pump mounted vertically to the inner crankcase by two studs, as on the C15G, just behind the timing-side main shaft. As on the twins, its driving spindle projected upwards to take a helical gear, driven clockwise by a worm on the crank behind the timing pinion. The 'S-type' feed pump gears were actually deeper than the B44's. However, all this was very necessary to provide both pressure and volume of oil flow healthy enough to service the plain big ends, and unfortunately the alloy body of the pump would prove vulnerable to over-tightening on its mountings, causing a stiffened-up pump, damage to the spindle gear, and a reduced flow to the vulnerable big end. In addition, the pump's spindle gear proved prone to wear due to the very small contact area of each tooth.

Other weaknesses in the system that remained were the wide-mesh sump filter and the rather vulnerable ball and spring pressure relief valve situated at the front of the right crankcase. The engine breathed via a hole in the outer bush of the hollow camshaft into a cavity between the inner and outer timing covers, and then went to atmosphere via a short pipe which came out on top of the gearbox. This breather system worked well as long as the sump was scavenging properly and the piston and barrel were in good condition.

The model's electrics were usefully uprated to 12 volts, with an RM19 alternator, independent coil, and Zener diode under the tank nose. Overcharging problems became a thing of the past, but the alternator proved vulnerable, as on its left end the relatively soft crankshaft forging was not really strong enough around the alternator's rotor keyway. The main body of the rotor could also loosen on its central steel boss. Chatter could then develop, which destroyed the rotor keyway and ultimately the crankshaft.

The model started out with 4CA contact breaker points. For smooth running, both the points and the advance-retard mechanism had to be spot on,

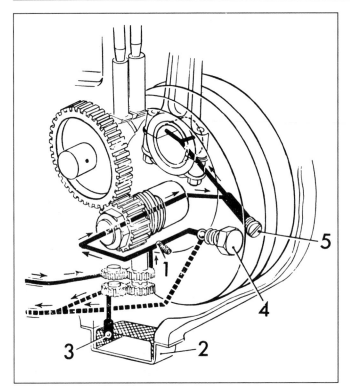

Oil circulation was crucial for the health of the plain big end bearing.

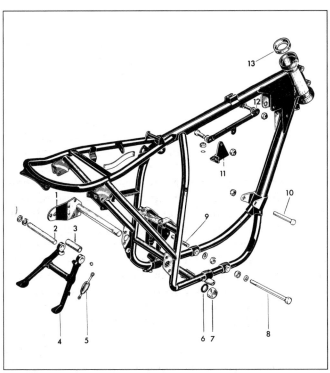

C25/B25's superior chassis.

and when they became less so, roughness under acceleration and 'hunting' at tickover were the early signs of trouble. To help time the ignition, BSA provided a pointer on the inside of the primary chaincase, which used together with a marker on the alternator rotor, was intended to give accurate setting by strobe light via the primary chaincase cover. Unfortunately, some of these markings were inaccurate and also, according to Tony Jones, further inaccuracies crept in due to the wear in the keyways and loosening of the rotor mentioned above.

This engine had a claimed output of 25 bhp, though the claim was dropped to 24 soon afterwards. Far from unflawed, it went in a chassis that was in many ways a big improvement on its predecessor. The frame was based on that of the works scramblers. The rear sub-frame was no longer bolted on, but gusseted where it was welded on to the bottom of the duplex bottom cradle tubes under the engine, with the swinging-arm fork mounted on the gusset plates. The swinging-arm pivoted now on rubber-bonded bushes, which when the time came were very hard to remove. Where the C15's top frame loop had continued in one loop at the rear to its bottom cradle, the C25's loop supported duplex tubes which splayed outwards to form complete loops with the bottom cradle tubes. Finally, the steering head angle was reduced from the C15's to 63°, with the previous weak steering head now massively gusseted on the top rail. The frame had a slightly longer wheelbase at 52 in and a 31 in seat height, which some found awkward when stationary, but which gave an undeniably big bike feeling.

This superior chassis rode at the front on a pair of forks with double damping by rod which had been developed by Jeff Smith, though the C25's version lacked gaiters, and its lower end differed from the Victor's in having wheel attachment by fork clamps rather than a pull-out spindle. At the rear there were Girling units, adjustable now, with partially exposed chrome springs, beneath chromed top covers. Wheels were 18 in, 3.25 front, 3.50 rear. A good bonus was that the rear one reverted to a sound qd design. Both front and rear brakes were 7 in, the front being an SLS design in a single-sided hub, and together they provided a respectably improved stopping distance of 30 ft from 30 mph.

The whole machine had been restyled with the American market in view. A separate chromed headlamp, shallower than the Sportsman's, was topped by the speedometer (there were no matching rev counters yet, a bad omission on an essentially high-revving machine). Mudguards were chromed blades with U-shaped tubular stays, and the rear one carried a new cast light alloy tail-light unit. The petrol tank was boldly sculpted in fibreglass with scalloped knee recesses, and strikingly finished in Bushfire Orange with white panels. It carried a hinged, snap-shut cap and the pear-shaped badges, and it only held $1^3/4$ gallons. The tank was echoed by a new shaped oil tank cover and matching side-panel, also in orange fibreglass. The oil tank itself had its contents increased from 4 to 5 pints. Topped by a new black 'humpy rump' seat with chrome trim, its pull-back handlebars finished with new bulbous cushioned grips, the C25 was a smart machine. A final practical bonus was that the previous skimpy rear chain had been enlarged to $5/8$ x $1/4$ in dimensions.

1967 also saw the deliveries of the B40 GB (WD). This model featured several changes from its civilian predecessor, most of them for the good. The bottom end was the strong G-series type. The army required the engine to be able to keep slogging away under heavy load and cross-country if necessary, so the model's gearbox featured trials gearing off the former C15T (so again, not with the later stub-tooth form gears), and trials tyres were fitted. The petrol tank was enlarged to 3½ gallons. The frame was the scrambles-derived type with all-welded sub-frame, and the strong, gaitered forks were two-way damped and of the BSA pattern, with fork end solid and the spindle threaded through it. Brakes were single-sided and 7 in, the rear wheel was qd, the rear sprocket bolt-on, the front wheel 20 in, mudguarding skimpier than the old civilian models, and the oil tank uncovered, as was the battery for the 12 volt electrics. The toolbox was, thankfully, hinged. The still skimpy rear chain was fully enclosed and the wheel bearings sealed. The headlamp was separate and carried the speedometer and rotary-action switches.

Compression was dropped to 7:1 to suit 80–90 octane military fuel, but despite this an exhaust valve lifter was fitted. Internally the roller big end bearing was retained, while a heavy-duty roller main bearing was fitted on the drive side. Both oil and air filtration came in for attention, with a paper motocross-type air element carried within the left-side compartment under a wire grille, and a Vokes-type filter with replaceable cartridge element fitted in the oil return line. A special small Amal carburettor was fitted, adapted from a stationary engine, with a butterfly valve operation designed to avoid sticking and to be completely watertight; it was not well liked. While good for 65 mph flat out, and capable of sustained slogging, the WD B40 models were quite heavy at around 350 lb kerbside.

Over the following three years an overseas version of this B40, the Rough Rider, was also produced both for military export orders and as a civilian

Leaping Redcaps on B40GB (WD) 350s.

model for agricultural use, like the Bantam Bushman. It featured full-width hubs fitted to Triumph-type forks with detachable end caps, no rear chain enclosure, a Concentric carburettor, plus a separate speedometer and a headlamp shell with a single flick-switch for the lights, while the ignition switch was beneath the seat.

Remarks

The C25's handling was in another league from the C15, braking was improved, the 12 volt electrics gave good lights and more reliability, and the powerful engine provided a fast, lively ride. But as already described, the C25's debut was fairly disastrous, as the high state of tune needed an experienced rider to walk the line between knocking the engine to pieces by the persistent use of low revs, and blowing it up by over-exploiting this 250's revvy nature — this bike could rev to 8,250 rpm, reach 55 mph in second, and 72 in third and still carried no rev counter. Factor in the fragile con rods and still vulnerable timing side bearing and oil pump, and it spelt serious trouble. At £249 it was £43 dearer than the C15, and weighed 35 lb more at 315 lb dry. This was a raw machine, vibratory, noisy mechanically, and with a raucous exhaust.

The B40 WD sounds like a good practical proposition, and was so when new, but given our stingy civil servants, army bikes were forced to go round the clock two and sometimes three times, and ended up fairly well clapped out, though much can be put to rights if you are so inclined.

1968

The C25 became the B25 Starfire and celebrated with a change of finish to Nutley Blue, with Ivory panels on the petrol tank. From April, the tank badges were made from new, anodized, ribbed moulding in light alloy, which couldn't split like their plastic predecessors. There was a new SLS 7 in brake with a full-width hub and in April a new method of clamping the bolt-on fork end caps. BSA had merged the US and the shrinking UK range, so there were now clipless gaiters on the front forks, higher rise handlebars, and side reflectors under the nose and on the side of the tail light unit. From April again, the previous rotary switch in the headlamp was replaced by a toggle one. The gearbox filler plug was now provided with a dipstick. A 35 amp fuse went in the wiring by the battery.

Internally, the feet of the tappets were deepened, a genuine improvement, and the clutch housing and chainwheel assembly were modified. The new items had grooves in the raised portion behind the chainwheel teeth. From engine No. B25 1042X, the 4CA contact breaker points were replaced by the superior 6CA which provided a fine adjustment facility. These are readily interchangeable with the previous ones. From around July 1967 there was a new rocker box assembly, so that the method of adjusting the tappets was reversed, ie the rocker spindles were turned inwards (towards each other) instead of outwards as previously. Rocker end float had always been controlled by thrust washers, Thackeray spring types on the C25, and these changes meant that there are two different rocker lengths.

1968 also saw the introduction of the Triumph version of the 250, the TR25W Trophy, mostly for the export market at first where trail bikes were

already established. It was cleverly styled to give a distinct identity with a long, red, angular 3¼ gallon steel petrol tank, and the Triumph name cast on the primary chaincase and the rocker inspection plate. Triangular black fibreglass side panels were also different in shape from the B25s, and the mudguards were painted. The seats had a ribbed top and no hump.

The separate chrome headlamp was smaller at 5½ in diameter, with a toggle light switch and an impractical push-pull dipswitch. The exhaust system was high level, mounted above the crankcase on the right and curling inside the frame before terminating in a shorty 'shotgun' silencer, protected by a chevron heat-shield plate, and emitting a very loud noise indeed. The shuttle valve front fork, soon to be adopted by the BSAs, came off the Tiger 90 350 twin, and was gaitered. It worked excellently.

A bash plate was fitted under the engine at the front. Seat height was 32 in and ground clearance was 8 in, both 1 in up on the B25, and folding footrests emphasized this Trophy's dual-purpose role. No centre stand was fitted. There was a 3.25 x 19 in front wheel with a fat 4 x 18 in cover on the qd rear wheel. High bars gave a comfortable riding position.

The engine was as the B25, but gearing was lowered even further by the simple expedient of replacing the standard 49-tooth rear sprocket by a 52-tooth item, and the 16-tooth gearbox sprocket with a 15-tooth one, on all but the earliest models. Claimed output was 22 bhp, and this didn't lower the top speed too much (81 mph on test), but it did mean that riders tended to rev the engine even harder, and wear it out even faster than the B25. There was also a military/police version of the TR25W which came with 8:1 compression, as well as fully valanced mudguards and shrouded rear units, plus a full-flow filter on the oil return line.

Remarks
The pity of it was that both the B25 and TR25W were great fun to ride, before oil leaks sprang from the gasketless outside joint faces or elsewhere, vibration got to the electrics, or the engine succumbed to one of the design weak points.

Left 1968, first year for the Triumph-badged and styled TR25W 250 Trophy.

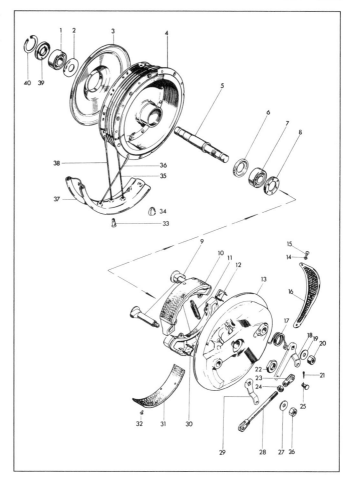

Right The excellent 7 in twin leading shoe front brake fitted to the roadster singles for 1969–70.

1969

There were a great many changes this year, which can sometimes make tedious reading but which can also make the difference between getting the right or wrong part at an autojumble. The blizzard of changes was led off by a couple of really good ones for the B25, the adoption of Triumph's excellent shuttle valve front forks, with Triumph-type lower members containing the two-way damped shuttle valves in the lower end of their stanchions; and of the 7 in 2LS brake in a full-width hub which they contained. Some considered this brake almost too potent for such a light machine and advised fitting a fork brace to prevent twisting, but it did reduce stopping distance from 30 mph to an impressive 28 ft. The fork was slightly shorter than the previous one, gave ½ in less movement at 5 in, increasing the wheelbase to 53 in and reducing ground clearance to 7 in. It worked very well indeed.

The petrol tanks and side panels became steel, the tank thankfully now had a capacity of 3¼ gallons and twin taps to provide a proper reserve, and thin rubber knee grips were added. A chromed grab rail was fitted. The dual seat was improved, with a perforated top. A stop light switch was fitted to the front brake cable, and a grease nipple fitted in the clutch cable casing, plus an adjuster mid-way in the front brake cable run. The contact breaker cover was now a polished casting carrying the BSA logo. The silencer's internals were revised to no very great effect, and the new internals required a two-layer gauze air filter and its appropriate case, plus a change of the Concentric's main jet to 180, or 170. The Concentric carburettor itself was modified to dispense with the detachable pilot jet.

Footrests became folding, with their rubbers of new material with a revised BSA logo. At engine No B25-3806, there had been a change to the centre stand; the latest type had a pivot bar and spacer, and could not go on previous machines. The springs on the rear units became fully exposed, and to match the new fork were modified to give ½ in less movement. Tubular connectors were welded to the steering head gusset plates to allow a fairing to be fitted. The valve lifter was deleted. And finally, a rev counter was offered as an option, driven by the worm in the timing side crankcase. This was a well-equipped machine, and claimed weight was down to 302lb.

On the electrical side, the alternator changed to the RM21, superior because it featured resin-encapsulated coils which were less liable to fragment. There was a new wiring harness with provision for capacitor ignition, a useful off-road, or indeed emergency, facility. In the headlamp, a previously red warning light for high beam now became green or blue. Internal changes were many, too. Late in the previous season, the problem of the shifting cylinder barrel liner had been addressed by the provision of a corrugated ring fitted on top of the liner flange in the head recess; these rings came in three sizes to suit individual engines. Tony Jones says that the problem with the liner is not frequently found today.

Within the gearbox, to help with more positive engagement of second, third and top, the camplate and lay shaft selector fork were modified to give more travel of the mainshaft slider when engaging top, and firmer indexing for third and second. At first the new camplate was marked '69' in place of the previous

1969 Starfire, well-equipped in the electrical and cycle departments.

'T', where it was marked at all, but then in January 1970 it reverted to the 'T' mark. Tony Jones recommends selective assembly where possible, and in any case to assemble and check the engagement of each gear in the cluster before fitting it into the crankcase.

1969 saw the factory attempt a transition from the various thread forms in the engine to Unified Thread for bolts, studs and screwed components. This led to some confusion as though the majority changed, the process was never completed; for instance, the rocker box fixings were not changed. But otherwise all 1/4 in diameter threads did change from BSC (26TPI) to the coarse UNC (20TPI). The thread for the hairpin spring anchor bolt also changed from 5/16 BSF to 5/16 UNC. The sump plate nuts became UNF and the fasteners for the outer and inner timing covers also obviously made the change to UNC.

Another sign that BSA was struggling with the model's problems was the fact that the width of the crankcase and primary chaincase join faces was increased by 15 per cent. While on the subject, it should also be mentioned that the cases had always been machined in pairs and should only be replaced as such, checking that the numbers underneath match.

In the clutch, the diameter of the clutch pinion operating spindle was increased from 0.342 to 0.403 in, with the outer cover modified accordingly. Either pair can go on any year. In the gearbox, the main bearing was moved 0.06 in nearer to the clutch, and the final drive gearbox sprocket's boss was made correspondingly shorter to maintain the same chain line.

The con rod was revised for the first of two times, with its bottom end made thicker and the little end bush dispensed with. For the Triumph twin's rod, which was also modified, the con rod bolts went to Unified Thread at the same time, but Tony Jones says this did not happen until the final 1971 change for the singles. The flywheels were modified to provide clearance for the stiffer rods. The method of crank fixing also altered; previously it had been fixed to the drive side ball bearing main, when the rotor nut was tightened. But in mid-year at engine No BC12468 the drive side's ball main bearing, a potential weak spot, was replaced by a roller bearing of the same dimensions, and therefore the timing side shaft was modified for the crank to lock to the ball bearing. Earlier shafts could be modified to suit by machining back on the timing side, and fitting an oil pump drive thrust washer there.

Also in mid-year, to counter wear the valve split collets and valve top collars were altered in length from previously, and featured a 20° inclusive angle instead of the previous 15°. They were interchangeable with the previous ones, but only as a set.

The TR25W got all the above engine and cycle part mods. In addition, its silencer became much larger and was fitted with a new chromed wire heat shield, with the exhaust pipe no longer tucked inside the frame but running back nearly straight from the top of the timing case. Though an improvement, it was not so stylish, and the exhaust note remained a noisy bark. The Triumph tank badges changed from the previous 'eyebrow' style to that year's square 'picture frame' type. The Triumphs had always had a grab rail, and now it changed to a hooped style, no longer attached to the rear lifting handles; and some machines came supplied with 18 rather than 19 in front wheels.

Left *BSA-owned subsidiary Motoplas produced functional if uncharismatic screens and plasticware, as on this C15 and later as on the B25 Fleetstar.*

Right *1970 B25 Starfire.*

1969 also saw a version of the 250 offered for corporate use by the police, couriers, etc. This was the B25FS Fleetstar. There had been a history of group use for the unit singles, with B40s previously supplied to the AA equipped with higher output RM15 alternators, bigger batteries, a heavy-duty rectifier, and a boost charge switch. Similarly, C15s had gone to the police with beefed up electrics. The Fleetstar would be supplied to 29 forces (perhaps largely because of the lack of any alternative light British motorcycle by now). Its most welcome feature was a drop in compression to 8.5:1. Claimed output was down to 21 bhp, and gearing was lowered by substituting a 52-tooth rear wheel sprocket for the B25's 47T. The cycle parts retained the more effective C15-type fully valanced mudguards, and top shrouded rear suspension units with black-painted springs.

The model was offered with a full range of equipment from BSA's subsidiary Motoplas, including legshields, crash bars, panniers, and a half-fairing. Finish for the civilian model was all black, with the petrol tank black and chrome with a white lining, a chromed headlamp and black mudguards with white pinstriping. The police models were similar but with their fork sleeves, side covers, mudguards and stays in white, and the petrol tank chrome with a white top lined in black. Like all police machines, they carried calibrated speedos, as well as legshields, Gazelle fairing, single seat and rear carrier.

Remarks

BSA did try and tackle the B25's problems, but the situation at the factory was increasingly chaotic, and blinkered marketing men probably militated against the de-tuning, ironically already partially available in the Fleetstar, which was the real necessary medicine. Meanwhile, in all but the engine department, the 1969-on B25 was a very nice motorcycle.

1970

There was another wave of detailed changes, some of which in retrospect seem odd in view of the complete redesign already underway for the following year. For the B25, the former oil tank side cover was discarded, with the left-hand

side panel reduced in size to match, and the oil tank filler cap repositioned to avoid the rider's leg. Both oil tank and side panel were now finished in black. On the handlebars, the front brake and clutch lever pivot blocks each included a ⁵/₁₆ in threaded hole for mirrors, a very good idea. The fork stanchions now had a hard chrome finish to increase oil seal life. The geometry of the prop stand spring attachment point was revised. In the headlamp, an oil pressure warning light was provided, though this could produce more false alarms than useful information. The silencers were redesigned again, becoming cigar-shaped, not so nice looking, but this time with genuinely quieter internals.

Internally, the camshaft engine breathers were modified to increase efficiency at the high revs these machines encouraged. This involved a new camshaft assembly and new timing marks. The previous marking was 'I', the 1970 mark 'V', and both were included on the new wheel until mid-year. This year also saw the contact-breaker bolt, which was part of the assembly, being modified to Unified Threads. So, confusingly, there was an interim camshaft assembly (Triumph part No E11124) with the improved breathing and altered marking, but without the Unified Thread bolt, though this could be added to it later. The final assembly was E11276. If putting a 1970 model year engine together, watch out not to time it to the 'I' mark, or the inlet valve can strike and damage the piston crown.

Tony Jones points out that the breathing system had always been a prime cause of oil leaks, as it could become overloaded by excessive crankcase pressure caused by wear or damage to the piston and barrel, by incorrect new piston rings, or a glazed bore, or occasionally by a loose exhaust valve guide. Another part of the system which was also modified was the crankcase pressure relief valve. Extra space was now made in the previous location to fit the superior Triumph twin-type assembled piston-type unit in place of the previous ball and spring.

The top piston ring changed from a plain compression type to a tapered ring like the middle one. In the clutch, there was an improved method of locating the spring cups in the clutch pressure plate, which was modified to suit. The sump filter became detachable from the sump plate, and thus easier to clean or renew. A smaller Lucas ignition coil was fitted. The carburettor was now rubber-mounted with the flange altered accordingly, and within the Concentric there was a redesigned needle jet holder, needle jet, and needle. The wiring harness now had provision for fitting direction indicators.

Late in the year came the most significant change to the lubrication system, with the adoption of an iron-bodied oil pump fastened by three studs, as found on the BSA twins. It was similar in appearance to the alloy pump, and as had been the case with the 1970 alloy pump the driven spindle now spigoted into the top cover, and while the driving spindle still spigoted to the scavenge gear, the top/body sections of the casing were dowelled for more accurate location, and with the new material it was no longer prone to distortion. The three-stud iron pump can be retro-fitted to earlier models subject to simple checks on the two-stud crankcases and a little work if necessary (see P.149).

The TR25W took on all the engine changes, as well as deleting its own triangular oil tank cover, and adopting its own new left-hand cover, now in steel. There was also a third change to the exhaust system in three years, with this one still high-level but running to the left of the machine, with the pipe and large silencer now shrouded by an unsightly grey moulded fibreglass cover attached by three screws.

Finally for all models in mid-year, as a matter of urgency, the previous bent wire clip for the front brake cable at the rear of the right-hand fork leg was replaced by a plastic guide. This was to prevent the cable bend which formed when the fork went to full compression, from snagging on the front mudguard bridge stay lug bolt, jerking the brake on and having the rider off. Naturally, it's not a bad idea to retro-fit.

Remarks
The 1970 250s, like those of the year before, are quite desirable motorcycles, despite the problems which remained with the engine. Fitting the iron-bodied, three-stud oil pump late in the season was the year's really vital development.

1971
This year saw the last act for BSA, with a completely restyled range. For the unit singles, this meant a new oil-bearing frame, alloy forks and trail bike style.

Below left The two-stud alloy oil pump, replaced by the superior three-stud cast iron pump late in 1970.

Below right 1971 BSA 'Gold Star' 250SS, the oil-in-frame 250 in street scrambler guise.

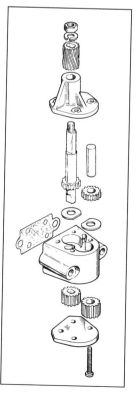

Both BSA and Triumph 250s were offered in street scrambler or trail versions, as the B25SS Gold Star/B25T Victor Trail/B25FS Fleetstar, or the Triumph T25SS Blazer/T25T Trail Blazer. These machines may have seemed somewhat incongruous at a time before the notion of trail bikes had really taken on in the UK, but their engines embodied a good many real improvements, which went some way towards tackling the 250's problems.

The new oil-bearing frame was based upon the Mk IV BSA works motocross chassis, and carried 4 pints of oil, one less than the Starfire. For the 1971 BSAs, the frame was finished in Dove Grey, in a feeble attempt to mimic the Rickman scrambler frame's nickel-plated finish; the Triumph's frame was black. Of the BSA it was said that it 'gave the model a second-hand appearance before it ever got dirty'. The chassis had a massive 2¼ x 14 in gauge top tube, and the oil was carried in this, in the tank rail, and in the single front down tube, which had a filter at its base. There was also, at last, a full-flow filter unit with replaceable paper element (every 4,000 miles was the recommended interval), mounted behind the gearbox in the oil return line. There was also a detail improvement to the feed line non-return valve, which was now held in by a bolt rather than the previous grub screw. The frame's oil filler cap was awkwardly located just behind the steering head.

Beneath the engine ran a twin tube engine cradle, and the rear sub-frame was of welded construction. The swinging-arm pivoted on needle races, which were very awkward to remove when the time came. The arm passed between lugs welded to the seat tube; also, unusually, the swinging-arm itself carried

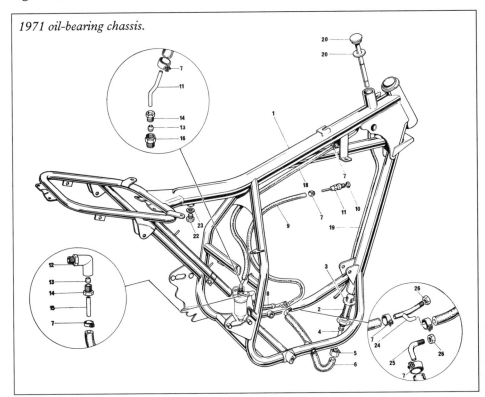

1971 oil-bearing chassis.

the pillion footrests. Rear chain tension could be set accurately on both sides by snail cam adjusters, just as well in view of the minimal chain's ability to stretch quickly.

The steering head bearings were a pair of Timken needle rollers, and the forks that pivoted on them had internal springs, alloy sliders and exposed, ungaitered, precision-ground, hard-chromed stanchions. They were supple, comfortable, and with 6¾ in of movement, useful on off-road trails. Their only drawback was that their aluminium sliders bore directly upon the stanchions, and hence could not be rebushed, but in operation wear proved to be minimal. The exposed stanchions did let dirt into the oil seals though, and quickly caused leaks.

The oil-in-frames were tall bikes, with a 32 in seat height, whether in SS form on 18 in wheels, or Trail with a 20 in front wheel. But the narrow nose of the comfortable black dual seat meant that getting one's feet down at rest was no problem for most. They were a little larger overall than the Starfire, with a 54 in wheelbase, and ground clearance of either 7 in or 7½ in for the Trails. Tyre sizes for the SS were 3.25 x 18 in front, and 3.50 x 18 in rear, while the Trail versions had a skinny 3 x 20 in front, and a chunky 4 x 18 in rear. The Trail had a sprung front mudguard which was fixed high up to the bottom of the lower fork crown, while the SS models had a conventional low-mounted unsprung guard, supported by a wire, rubber-mounted cross stay on each side. These stays would prove very vulnerable to fracturing.

The wheels contained new alloy conical-hub brakes. The SS had an 8 in TLS front and 7 in SLS rear, as on the Group's twins, while the Trail had a 6 in SLS front which was not really effective enough on the road. Despite this, it was offered on the export B25SS. The rear wheels were sadly no longer qd, and fiddly to remove. On the 8 in front brake there was an air scoop, though this tended to allow the drum to fill with rain water. Adjustment of the brake shoe pivots was offered via the Lockheed-designed, click-stop Micam system, with the adjusters reached by a screwdriver via a hole beneath a rubber plug in the conical face of the hub; just as well, since frequent adjustment was necessary to maintain good braking. The brake plates on the Trail versions were painted black, on the SS anodized silver.

The brakes' problems were partly because they featured an alloy hub but steel brake shoes, and different rates of expansion meant that the hub expanded away from the shoes when it got hot under hard operation. The other problem was that the brakes' two cam operating levers, which themselves were rather too short to provide optimum leverage, were operated by the cable, with the nipple end pulling the front lever on, while the cable's casing 'pushed' the rear lever. But in operation, the cable casing, which was wound wire beneath its PVC casing, compressed like a spring, and finally would become squeezed up and lose power. Fitting a spring on the exposed portion of cable between the two levers, as Triumph soon did on their twins, can help to keep the cable properly seated on the levers. In practice with the SS singles, which weighed in at just 290 lb, the brakes worked well enough if kept fettled to maintain the 28 ft stopping distance at 30 mph of their predecessors.

Electrical arrangements on the new models were distinctive. The alternator was a Lucas RM21, direction indicators were fitted as standard on both versions, and the bulk of the equipment went in a single light alloy 'black box' under the front of the petrol tank. This carried the ignition switch on its left

Bizarre-looking box-type silencer found on the new oil-in-frame unit singles.

side, as well as the reflectors required by US legislation. Inside it were the coil, Zener diode, rectifier, direction indicator relay, and 2MC capacitor which was standard, so that machines could be ridden off-road with headlamp and battery removed. A nine-pin plug and socket connection at the rear of the box allowed the headlamp, indicators and warning lights (now main beam, pilot, indicators and oil pressure warning) to be instantly detached. The only problem with this compact arrangement was that the forward position of the box and the narrowness of the standard tiny tanks both made it and its contents pretty vulnerable to rain.

For the standard, petrol tank size was a puny 1³/₈ gallon which, combined with overall mpg now down to around 65, only gave a range of less than 80 miles before having to go on reserve. The SS tank was in steel with a conventional twist-on cap; the Trail in alloy, with a hinged-on job. There was also an optional steel 3 gallon tank for the BSA, in a rather ugly style with knee grips and a squared off hump at the back.

Finishes for the SS models were the grey frame, Flamboyant Red, or blue, for the mudguards and side panels, and as base colour for the petrol tank, which had a diagonal gold-lined black stripe. The BSA Trail model's tank was in plain polished alloy with the gold-lined black stripe, carrying gold BSA transfers, and its mudguards were chromed. The Triumph T25SS/T25T was distinct, with black cycle parts, the mudguards a different style from the BSA version, and painted red with a gold-lined black centre stripe, the side panels black, and the handsome 2 gallon steel petrol tank red with gold-lined swept-back scallops above the gold-lined black Triumph transfer. Headlamps for all were chromed, with a twist-action main beam switch, and were carried on shaped brackets of chromed steel rod, rubber mounted from the upper and lower fork yokes. As mentioned these brackets were very prone to fracture. The tail lights, with pointed 'teat' type lenses, were carried on a crudely extended pressed tin mounting block.

Right New 8 in twin leading shoe front brake in conical hub, with air scoop. Operating mechanism was flawed.

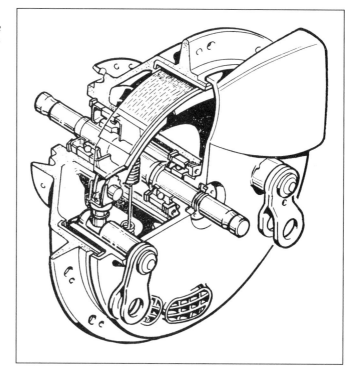

Below Nicely styled Trail version of the last Triumph 250, the T25T, in a rural setting.

Another style feature was the exhaust system, which was matt black and very distinctive, with the pipe, which was simply a push fit into the head, snaking back above the timing-side crankcase, to join the odd-looking black lozenge-shaped box silencer angling upwards and backwards until it was level with the base of the dual seat, where it sprouted a small tail-pipe. The main body of the silencer was incongruously covered by a chromed heat shield with circular perforations, while the pipe got its own little bolt-on shield, but which was less conspicuous in black. In practice, the silencer emitted a pleasant, deep muted burr which rose to a snarl under acceleration, but did keep the decibels down.

There was a grab-rail at the rear and high bars at the front, braced on the Trail versions, with a new set of Lucas alloy-bodied controls built into the control blocks. The thumb switches on these were too short, and the housings vulnerable to water. A rev counter to match the rubber-mounted speedo was optional; for the SS models both instruments were of a smaller 60 mm diameter, while for the Trail they were 80 mm, the same as the B25's new big brother, the 500 cc B50. Both versions emphasized their dual role by coming equipped with a bash plate under the front of the sump, and forward-tilted folding footrests.

Within these new cycle parts, the engine had come in for considerable attention. The wider rear mounting lug has already been mentioned. Claimed output was down to a more realistic 22.5 bhp at 8,250 rpm. The single most important change was to the con rods, which for the second time were thickened, with a big end boss $^1/_8$ in bigger than previously, and this time strengthened effectively. Their special waisted cap nut bolts and engineering grade self-locking nuts were $2^1/_2$ in long and changed from Cycle to Unified Thread, with the torque figure reduced accordingly. These rods could and should be retro-fitted to other B25s, through it's a job for professionals as the flywheels were again modified to provide clearance for the stiffer rod, and the crank's balance factor reduced from 58 per cent to 54 per cent. The crankshaft itself was slightly shorter than the earlier one, again a bonus as it means that it can be shimmed in to fit all the earlier crankcases.

Another improvement was the fitting of superior Nimonic 80 exhaust valves marked N80 on their stems, and interchangeable with previous versions. The valve stems and guides were also, finally, modified. The guides were now flanged, where the earlier ones had been stepped to provide better location, very important in view of the damage to head and piston if a valve dropped. Valve stems had also tended to ridge near the top and bottom of their travel, and guides to wear at the same place. The new guides were not readily interchangeable with the old unless the hole for the guide in the earlier head was counter-bored to receive the flange. The 1971 head also featured rocker box studs of $^5/_{16}$ in diameter rather than the previous $^1/_4$ in. Studs centres too were modified to give more material for the bosses, so the new rocker boxes can only be used with the new head, but as a pair they will fit all years. The main joint faces were wider than previous, but used the same size copper gasket as before.

At the other end of the cylinder, the size of the base flange was increased, with the related parts modified. The 1971 cylinder base gasket, previously only paper, was a slightly thicker material, and this led to a slight drop in compression.

The clutch chainwheel was altered and the clutch centre was redesigned, losing its previous lip at the back but gaining a stiffer pressure plate, an extra fifth friction plate, and a clutch bearing thrust washer on an enlarged hub. The latter should not be omitted, or spring pressure is transferred to the small flange on the keyed hub, by direct contact with the drum. At OTJ today they also usually insert an extra steel plate next to the pressure plate, to compensate for the thinner linings on replacement friction plates. Otherwise the spring cups can bottom in the clutch centre, instead of bearing down on the pressure plate, meaning no drive at all! In the gearbox on the SS models a 17-tooth gearbox sprocket was adopted to raise gearing, though the Trail model retained lower gearing with the previous 16-tooth. All used a 52-tooth rear sprocket, and gearing can be raised again for an easier, less vibratory ride around the 60 mph mark (and also mpg increased to 75) by substituting the B50's 47-tooth item, easy enough since the rear sprockets were bolt-on.

The camshaft gained the narrower B 50 type camwheel and a thrust washer at its outer end to improve location and reduce wear. The camshaft timing mark changed from the previous confusing 'V' and 'I' to just the 'I' on each camwheel for alignment. In mid-year there were some modifications. From engine No XE2578 B25T there was a new pressure-release valve assembly, identified by '75' stamped on the domed cap, set to release pressure at 75 psi. All existing 1971 models were strongly recommended to be so modified, using spring No 70–791. Another factory recommendation was to drill a $^1/_{16}$ in hole

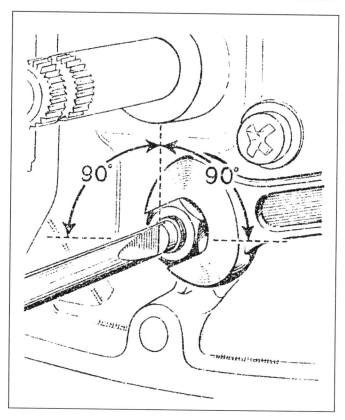

Some B25/T25s had this facility for gearchange quadrant adjustment.

in the base of the contact-breaker housing to allow the release of condensation. Finally, some 250s had provision for adjustment of the gearchange quadrant to ensure positive gear selection. The gearchange return spring anchor on them incorporated an eccentric spindle and lock nut where it fitted the eye of the spring. At rest, the rider could select one gear at a time, and turn this adjuster until it was possible to select positively. However, OTJ's experience has been that this was rarely necessary unless the gearchange spring was out of shape already. Finally, the factory eventually recommended that the rear chain oiler from the primary chaincase be removed and blanked off, something Tony Jones endorses as all it really did was harmfully deplete the oil in the chaincase.

In addition to the six 250 variants described, there was also an OIF version of the Fleetstar, with an 8.5:1 compression piston which is a useful retro-fit for any B25.

Remarks

The new models, though doomed by BSA's situation, had quite a lot to offer. They were comfortable and fun to ride, either on trails or in town, though perhaps not for long distances. When your riding style had been adapted to suit the tall build and high bars, they could be swung exuberantly through bends, and held the road very well. Excellent power to weight ratio gave an overall top speed of around 87 mph on the SS versions, but vibration from the rattly engine in a light frame normally became an inhibiting factor before that. Their small turning circle was a boon both in town and on the trail, and off road, though rather too heavy to be a serious enduro tool, their low-speed stability was exceptional, traction in mud very good, behaviour in slime predictable, and yet they also had enough poke to blast up stony hills; and once again, they were fun. Good lights, comfort, reasonable brakes, and pizzazz — these 250s did have an appeal. They would never be a restful ride, but they could be exhilarating.

Niggles included the fact that clutch take-up and transmission were sharp, they were rather easy to stall in traffic, and difficult to restart when hot. They

went out of tune quickly, with the contact breakers requiring frequent attention. The side panels, fastened now by push-and-turn fasteners into bent-wire
housings, fell off quite easily. The combination of vibration and poor welding
meant that a B25SS on test with *Bike* magazine had all four of its mudguard
stay ends shear, as well as the wire headlamp mounting. In addition, the fork
oil seals leaked badly and the Lucas winkers were their usual troublesome and
erratic selves. The silencer's very individual shape meant that only a special
proprietary rack could be fitted for luggage. The push-fit exhausts leaked,
causing backfires. None of the Trails, and only some of the SS models, fitted
centre stands, which made adjusting the rear chain with those useful snail-
cams a two-man job. The lack of a qd wheel was a minus point, as was the
ineffective front mudguard.

The improved con rod, oil pump and oil filtration, were all in these
machines' favour, but the US-oriented styling didn't suit everyone, and the
OIF arrangement itself could be a drawback, as the 4 pint capacity was minimal, meaning hot running (though fitting an oil cooler can both help that, and
give an extra pint). More fundamentally, any major engine blow-up, never too
far away with these 250s, could allow large lumps inside the chassis where they
would lurk, ready to do fresh damage.

A few of the BSA's 250s continued to be produced into the early part of
1972 until April, now with black frames and black front brake plates, and most
often the blue finish. Then the end came for the 250 line.

C15/B40/B25 today

The unit 250s and 350s evolved so radically during their 13 full years of production that the first job today is deciding which of the sometimes very different models would suit your requirements, and likes and dislikes. Broadly, I
would say that if you're new to old bikes some of the earlier models suit best.
Since the 250 learner limit no longer applies, the B40, and especially a 1965
side-points B40, makes the best sense.

Left *Nicely restored
B25SS in non-
standard colour scheme,
but with black frame
indicating a probable
late model.*

Right *Best C15, the
1966 C15G series.*

Though finding one at the right price may be a problem, as they are now sought-after for adaptation to pre-'65 Trials, they do have usefully increased performance, better handling with a stiffer frame and heavier forks, and a rather less stressed engine, than the 250. As mentioned, the later WD B40s will have had hard lives, but if you can find one that has already had work done on it competently, the specification is very tempting. Otherwise one of the far more common 1965–7 C15F or C15G 250s is the ticket.

If, however, you (a) consider yourself a competent mechanic with some experience in the old bike field, and (b) like to ride relatively fast, the later B25s, approached with caution, have a lot to offer for the money (£750–800 should get you something decent). On balance I would go for a '69–'70 B25 or TR25W, as although the oil-in-frame SS machines' engines had some desirable features, these can be retro-fitted to the earlier models (though at a price), and as road-going motorcycles the oif bikes are a little less practical — though if you live somewhere with regular access to green lanes and fields, their dual-purpose trail capability might swing the balance in their favour.

You can't be involved with one of these machines for long without running across the name OTJ. That stands for Olive and Tony Jones, who run a very comprehensive business indeed providing spares, service and innovations for the unit single engines; the engines only, it should be noted, not the cycle parts. OTJ themselves were in fact at first unwilling to work on B25 engines, but now, claims Tony Jones, 'when they leave us they are just as reliable as other models', the secret being simply very careful assembly of all elements; this does reinforce the caveat on inexperienced mechanics tackling this particular high-performance model. OTJ will undertake as much or as little of the work as you wish, including fitting a new crank, con rod or bearing and leaving you to assemble the rest of the engine. As mentioned earlier, though the work is to a high standard it cannot be expected to be cheap, so ideally try to find a machine which has already had some of it done!

Two pieces of work seem to me essential, whichever model you settle on. The first is replacing the points with an electronic ignition system. Luckily OTJ now supply these for distributor as well as side-points models. For the side-points, either the Boyer or Lucas Rita systems will do, with the Rita around £40 dearer at about £85, but with some replaceable components. If it's for a C15, these systems used to require an uprate to 12 volts, with appropriate bulbs, Zener diode, etc, so the total cost was up around the £200 mark, but now 6 volt electronic kits are available. The set-and-forget systems eliminate a big niggle from life with a unit single, and a full 12 volt system provides not only better lights, but also an end to overcharging.

The second essential job for all is the fitting of a full-flow oil filter cartridge kit on the return line, as already found on the B25SS and on WD B40s. Such filters, whether standard or after-market, should be renewed about every 4,000 miles.

For a C15 or B40, though less temperamental than the B25, there will probably be some problems. Top of the list must come the gearbox; naturally, if it ain't broke, don't fix it, but as Tony Jones has said, 'The gearbox is possibly the area of most difficulty to many owners, and we find that parts are often replaced either unnecessarily or in isolation when the problem relates to several components.' In a previous existence Tony was a civil engineer specializing

The later 250s, like this 1971 T25T, needed plenty of adjustments. Simplify one area by fitting electronic ignition.

in motorways, and this shows in the meticulously methodical approach OTJ take to problems. Four pages of their large catalogue (currently priced at £2) are devoted to the gearbox, and not only provide a checklist of around 150 relevant items, all cross-referenced to the 1,200 item price list, but also a table of the 11 major variations in gears and clusters over the years among the different models, with keyed to the table an accompanying diagram of parts. OTJ also, among other sub-assembly repair services, offer one on the box. They are happy to give advice on this or other problems, but prefer to do so over the telephone, as it is hard to keep up with the volume of written replies to home and abroad.

C15/B40 gearbox problems can centre around the gear selection mechanism, for the actual bearings and shafts were quite long lived. As mentioned, the tell-tale is a dangling gear pedal, for the thin splines on the shaft let go if the clamp is left loose, and the answer is fitting a new or exchange gearchange shaft mechanism, with a new pedal if necessary (it's the same as the Cub's). Clutch pushrods were also a problem area. Another possible trouble spot on distributor models is damage to the splines at the sleeve gear end of the mainshaft, usually caused by lack of adequate lubrication. Another one to watch is the danger of losing all the gearbox oil due to faulty mating of the kickstart spindle and case. No seal was fitted there, but Tony Jones believes leakage is usually due to a high oil level and to wear on the spindle where it runs in the inner timing cover. Oil leaks in this area generally can be due to the crankcase breather being overloaded, since it vents into the cavity between the inner and outer covers. You may care to consider extra breathing arrangements; an additional pipe from the top of the timing chest, from the tops of the rocker spindle inspection chest, from the front valve inspection cap, or from the primary chaincase side, any or all of these have been tried. OTJ also offer a definitive solution to the problem of the ineffective felt washer behind the oil seal in the gearbox sprocket cover. This is their 'outrigger kit', which features a sealed bearing that goes in the sprocket cover and provides a third bearing.

The kickstart mechanism problems have been mentioned, and particularly apply to the distributor models where the pawl set-up is small and prone to wear. In addition, the slot for the pawl may be worn or elongated so that the pawl pivots at an angle, and wears both itself and the ratchet track in lay shaft first gear. Replacement of the pawl, plunger and spring is the answer. If the two flats which engage with the return spring anchor plate are worn, the spring will keep trying to push the plate off the flats and jam the spindle. Finally, the larger B25 kickstart quadrant and bush can be retro-fitted on the earlier side-points models to advantage, with a little work.

There's more, but really the definitive fix in this area was provided in three articles by Tony Jones for *Classic Mechanics*, details of which will be found in the book section at the end of this chapter.

As mentioned, other C15 engine problems concerned pistons and rings, and here OTJ offer superior Cords rings, as well as pistons. Roller bearing big ends, and a needle roller replacement for the troubled plain timing side main bearing, are also part of the service.

On an everyday level, one good dodge for a C15/B40 — if you're not too bothered about originality and are using and servicing the bike regularly — is to replace the early machine's primary chaincase with one off a B25. These are available new (from Lightning Spares among others), and have the same fit and screws as the Ceefers. But they no longer used two of those screws, which inevitably quickly became worn, for both retaining the chaincase and checking the oil level or draining the oil. The B25 cover fitted a separate drain plug and an extra screw above the rim for the level. They also had two inspection caps in place of the C15's solitary one for the clutch centre, which means that you can check primary chain tension without removing the cover, as well as topping up the oil.

While on the primary side, the primary chaincase gasket is long, and to avoid oil leaks here, use grease on the gasket, and just a thin smear of jointing compound on the unthreaded part of the bolts (which can profitably be

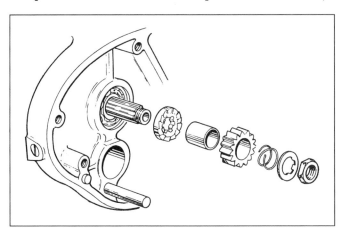

Kickstart ratchet assembly for the B25.

replaced with an Allen screw kit, as can the timing side cover screws) to prevent seepage. It is also a good idea to fit a primary chain tensioner to models before engine No C15S 3001/B40 2501, when they weren't yet fitted. However, this is one of several Ceefer components where, according to Tony Jones, you have to watch out for sub-standard pattern parts. Others include selector forks, gearchange shafts, oil pumps and their spindle gears, some B25 gears and various clutch parts.

The overly compliant C15 front fork might well benefit from new springs, and there's not a lot to be done about the 250's brakes as there were no later tweaks to substitute; just keep them in good condition and learn to anticipate. One of the most regular chores will be adjusting the skinny $^1\!/_2$ x $^5\!/_{16}$ in rear chain, which needs to be done at least every 1,200 miles. Engine oil changes for the 4 pint capacity Ceefer should be every 1,000 miles, religiously. After fiddling with the toolbox lid's hollow bolts a few times, you may well consider adapting them to take a simple cabinet lock, thus killing the two birds of security and convenience with one stone. Favourite tyres are the same excellent 17 in Avon Mk II Speedmaster front and SM rear as on the Cub. Plugs are Champion N5s, against N3s for the B25. Some approximate modern colour equivalents are as follows: for C15 Fuchsia Red (1958–63), try Vauxhall 230S, while for C15 Royal Red, it's Vauxhall Venetian Red BS2007. B40 Red, on the other hand, is said to be close to Jaguar Carman.

The B25/TR25W series (but not their SS successors) immediately demand two pieces of work if any peace of mind is to be had. First, if your machine pre-dates late 1970, you need the cast iron three-stud oil pump; aside from the fixing, for identification these were stamped 'S' (as against the B44's version which were stamped 'V' and differed internally with shallower feed pump gears). If you're fitting one of these to an earlier B25, the factory advised that the third fixing could not be used, and suggested removing part of the stiffening web from the inner side of the inner timing cover to prevent it fouling the pump, which was larger than the previous one. Before tightening the fixing stud nuts, you had to ensure that the pump was not being held off its seating by the pump spindle housing, which could foul the crankcase main bearing boss, and should be filed down if necessary. Once in place the distortion-resistant, cast-iron pump is a major factor in prolonging big end life. OTJ will rebuild your own or supply a new pump which they say is put together to closer tolerances than those specified by BSA for volume production.

The second essential piece of work is fitting a late-type con rod. CCM, the competition bike company who carried on developing the unit singles for sport to the end of the 1970s, offer a massively strong rod, or OTJ do a polished SS-type rod. Another option is the strong Triumph T100 Daytona 500 twin rod, whose changes followed that of the unit singles, but which lacks the oil-pressure relief drilling. Fitting these to either a '67/'68 engine or to '69/'70 is not entirely simple, as the flywheels for both have to be modified to provide clearance for the stiffer rod. The flywheels have to come off, and metal be taken from them close to the crankpin, an expert's job which if done properly will not require the crank to be rebalanced. Tony Jones says that the SS-type rod should give no trouble unless the big ends have been hammered into the ground, when the 'eye' may pull fractionally oval.

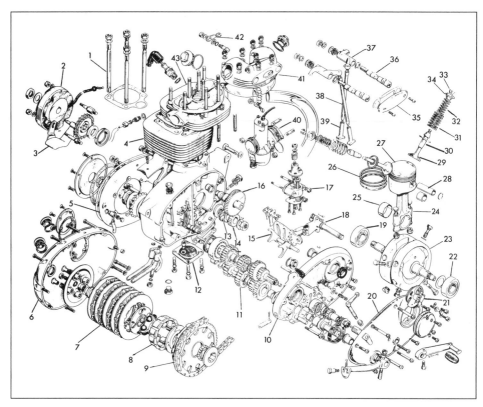

B25 engine exploded — as they sometimes did!

With the big ends, one way to go is the needle roller bearing assembly used in the '67-on WD B40. If you stay with the plain big end shells, the detachable end cap was a steel forging, and the eye was ground with this cap in position, a difficult job because of the two materials, hard steel and soft alloy, to be worked in one operation. Likewise, says Tony Jones, the relatively slim big end bearing means that regrinding the crank is another difficult job requiring a special narrow wheel set up for just one journal. Sounds like another one best left to the professionals. Of course an SS model has all this — oil pump, stronger rod — to begin with. (But even then they've been known to go bang...)

Tony Jones points out that BSA also made a quantity of complete B25SS crankcases (ie with bearings, seals, studs, etc) in 1971, but with a narrow lug at the back to enable them to be fitted as replacements on earlier models. They do not appear in any parts list but were No 71-8000, and OTJ have a few pairs. They can equally be used in an oil-in-frame with the addition of a simple tubular distance piece at the back.

Still on the major engine work front, uprating the 1967–9 drive side mains to 1970's roller is a good idea. But if undertaken, the crank has to be modified by reducing the projection of the boss for the timing side bearing from $^{29}/_{32}$ in to $^5/_8$ in, and fitting a spacer, No 41-0565. The crank is then located endways by the timing side bearing when the timing pinion nut is tightened, instead of by the drive side bearing as previously.

Another profitable area to work on is the valves. Valve stems tended to ridge near the top and bottom of their travel, with guide wear in the same locations. If play is excessive, both valve and guide need replacing, together with springs. As mentioned, there have been outsize valves available to counter inconsistencies in cylinder head valve seats, though supplies of these seem to have dried up. Don't neglect to renew the valve collars and collets, preferably with the improved 1970 type. Tony Jones points out that loose valve guides can be the cause of apparently inexplicable excess crankcase pressure, oil loss and lack of power.

Gearbox and clutch were another B25 problem department, despite being stronger than the C15's. Both worked very well when in good condition, but false neutrals and jumping out of second and third gear obtrude when wear sets in. If rebuilding, always replace the selector forks. OTJ supply a set of shims as part of a thrust washer and shims package for the gearbox, to move the third gear pinion closer to the sliding dog to give correct engagement. Though the camplate itself wears well, OTJ usually flatten the 'peaks' in the camplate's roller tracks slightly between top and third, and third and second, especially with '69-on models, to avoid contact halfway up the spring instead of at the bottom, because the clearance is very small there. The camplate spring itself also affects this and should be a continuous curve, not with a kink at the top as on some pattern items.

In the clutch, fitting the stiffer SS-type pressure plate is a good idea, but if you also then use an extra plate to avoid slip, clutch action becomes heavy and it is advisable to fit a heavy-duty cable.

The kickstart mechanism, while again more robust than the C15's, was far from perfect. Tony Jones advises checking the teeth on the quadrant and

The unit engines could be quite seriously fast, as exemplified by this 500 production class racer.

mainshaft pinion for wear, and changing the small mainshaft pinion before wear is transferred to the quadrant. Also check the ratchet ring which transfers drive from the pinion to the shaft, and replace the thin-gauge ratchet spring if it looks lop-sided. The steel bush in the outer timing cover wears little, but for reasons already mentioned, always renew the oil seal.

Piston ring condition in these engines is even more crucial due to their high-revving nature, and again the Cords rings, which consist of a number of thin heat-treated steel segments in each groove, have OTJ's approval. As does the substitution of the '68-on cam followers (tappets) with their thicker feet; both camshafts and followers are prone to rapid wear unless the lubrication system is in top shape. To this end OTJ favour the later easier-to-clean sump filter with detachable gauze, to which they add a magnetic filter underneath, a gasket either side of the gauze, and fasten the assembly with Allen screws instead of the standard studs. Fitting the pressure relief valve from a T140 can help increase pressure and improve the supply to the big end. Another simple aid to correct lubrication is taking care not to overfill the oil tank.

If you are working on your own engine, OTJ can supply a couple of special tools which are mandatory. One of them is a clutch extractor tool, not expensive, but essential. A final service I should mention of the many OTJ offer can have a very beneficial effect on the vibration associated with the B25 series. This is simply to drill out and re-sleeve with oversize sleeves the three engine mounting lugs, so that the mounting bolts locate the engine firmly. Simple, but they swear by it.

On an operational level, one of the B25's more irritating traits is difficulty in hot starting. Once your electronic ignition is in place to secure the timing, this will probably be due to the quite steeply downdraught carburettor, which makes flooding all too easy, especially if the bike is left on its side stand with the petrol tap still open. If it then won't go, switch off the petrol and ignition, close the throttle, and kick it over five or six times to clear the engine, and then try again. And when cold starting, don't forget to let the engine warm up for a

The level of equipment of oil-in-frame machines is seductive, and they make sense if you have access to field or trail.

minute or two before thrashing it, if you want reasonable life for the cams and followers.

If the catalogue of pitfalls has been a bit off-putting, perhaps we should emphasize the positive a little. B25s may never have achieved their mastermind's 100 mph target, but some of the works ones came damn close, and a stock engine put together lovingly should be good for nearly 90 — faster than a Honda Super Dream! — though if you're going for those exalted regions, first locate and fit a rev counter (OTJ supply a kit). Even with the lower compression Fleetstar piston which I would fit (but then I'm like that) they are still good for 80 mph, and the handling should match — John Grew's B25 racer in the 1989 Classic Manx was faster on the corners than a Ducati he was duelling with. These can be real street tools, but once again not if they're lugged in high gear, or ridden at really insensitively high revs. It's a fine line, but potentially a stimulating one, and for the '69–'70 machines, one with looks and brakes to match.

In conclusion, my most recent encounter with a unit single involved a brief run for *Classic Bike Guide* magazine on a rough but rideable £350 example, a 1966 C15G, no less, brush-painted turquoise, sporting a large Gold Star-type silencer and resurrected from Wales. This is what I found.

'Trying to ignore the long, long clutch cable waving around my left leg, I snicked down into first, and bumped away. The clutch was light, the gearchanges smooth and easy, and the little bike moved away briskly. There was good, unhesitating acceleration to an indicated mid-40 on the speedo. Into the bendy Cheshire lanes the handling at those speeds was very reassuring, with firm front forks and no reluctance to swing around corners, even those that smelled of pig but carried recent evidence of nearby dairy production.

'At that pace the 6 in brakes were OK too, with only around 300 lb kerbside to stop. The engine carried its own rev-limiter, beginning to vibrate noticeably at 50, as if querying the wisdom of holding it up there for too long. Over mixed going the 250 could be hustled along at a pace definitely comparable to a 350 heavyweight single of the same era; it just did it in a different way, a livelier, more aggressive, chirpier manner. Which would have suited the many young riders who started out on a C15.

'I enjoyed the bike on the empty, sunny lanes, but on nearby A-roads other traffic appeared behind with disconcerting swiftness, reminding you of how time has moved on and average speeds risen. And after a good whang through the gears on the A-road, taking it up to 60(!), once I'd turned for home and decided to play safe, at lower throttle openings the engine seemed to falter, or be just about to. Only when I opened it up again on the home straight was it instantly willing again, the big silencer giving a last flat bark.

'So — surprisingly engaging to ride, but with a hint of dodginess and lack of stamina. I could imagine using a C15 quite happily for a daily town-and-country commute, but preferably one of no more than 10 or 12 miles, if only because the seat seemed painfully hard after just a few miles. I don't think I'd ever come to love a Ceefer, but I could probably live with one.' Amen to that.

BSA C15 (1959): Technical Data

Engine

Bore (mm)	67
Stroke (mm)	70
Capacity (cc)	247
Compression ratio	7.25:1
Ignition	Battery/coil
Carburettor	$^7/_8$ in Amal Monobloc 375/34

Transmission
Sprockets

Engine	23
Clutch	52
Gearbox	17
Rear wheel	45
Top gear	5.985
3rd gear	7.649
2nd gear	10.54
1st gear	15.96

Chain front Duplex (in) $^3/_8$ x $^1/_4$, 68 pitches
Chain rear (in) $^1/_2$ x $^5/_{16}$, 113 pitches

Brakes

Diam x width front (in)	6 x 0.87
Diam x width rear (in)	6 x 0.87

Tyres

Size front (in)	3.25 x 17
Size rear (in)	3.25 x 17

Electrical

Battery	10 ah
Headlamp (diam in)	6
Voltage	6

Miscellaneous

Fuel Imp (gals)	$2^1/_2$
Seat height (in)	30
Width (in)	26
Length (in)	78
Ground clearance unladen (in)	5
Dry weight (lb)	280
Speedometer (mph)	80

Triumph TR25W Trophy (1968): Technical Data

Engine

Bore (mm)	67
Stroke (mm)	70
Capacity (cc)	247
Compression ratio	10:1
Ignition	Battery/coil
Carburettor	28 mm Amal Concentric 928

Transmission
Sprockets

Engine	23
Clutch	52
Gearbox	15
Rear wheel	52 (Early models 49)
Top gear	7.838
3rd gear	9.752
2nd gear	12.9
1st gear	20.79

Brakes

Diam x width front (in)	7 x $1^1/_8$
Diam x width rear (in)	7 x $1^1/_8$

Tyres (Trials Universal)

Size front (in)	3.50 x 19
Size rear (in)	4 x 18

Electrical

Battery	10 ah
Headlamp (diam in)	$5^1/_2$
Voltage	12

Miscellaneous

Fuel Imp (gals)	$3^1/_4$
Seat height (in)	32
Width (in)	28
Length (in)	82

	(Or with 49T rear chainwheel)		Ground clearance	
Top gear		7.386	unladen (in)	8½
3rd gear		9.189	Dry weight (lb)	320
2nd gear		12.16	Speedometer (mph)	120
1st gear		19.59		

Chain front Duplex (in) ³/₈ x ¼, 70 pitches   Chain rear (in) ⁵/₈ x ¼,   100 pitches

Engine and frame numbers

The frame number should be found stamped on the left-hand side of the front engine mounting lug, and the engine number on the left-hand side of the crank-case, just below the cylinder barrel. However, on some models the frame number is to be found either on the prop stand lug, or on the left side of the steering head.

To the end of 1968, BSA used one system of numbering for both engines and frames. However, engine and frame numbers seldom matched, and prefixes and suffixes denoting model year and type sometimes differed in an inconsistent way. Even without that factor, things can be complicated; the C15, for example, was built with appropriate suffix letter in nine models — US (a 'B' suffix), police (a 'P' suffix), sports (an 'R' suffix) or Pastoral (a 'T' engine suffix like the Trials, but an 'A' or 'E' frame suffix), and so on — all in more than one model year; and there were 22 Ceefer variants altogether.

If you happen to run across a unit engine with a 'CDE' or 'CD' suffix, grab it, as it could signify one of Jeff Smith's scramblers, a 'Competition Department Engine'.

The 1969 and later system is provided at the end.

	Engine	**Frame**
1959		
C15	C15-101	C15-101
1960		
C15	C15-11001	C15-11001
1961		
C15	C15-21251	C15-22001
SS80	C15SS-1101	C15-27644
B40	B40-101	B40-101
1962		
SS80	C15SS-1101	C15-31801
B40	B40-3601	B40-3511
SS90	B40BSS-101	B40-3511
1963		
C15	C15-41807	C15-38035
SS80	C15SS-2705	C15-38035
B40	B40-4506	B40-5017
SS90	B40SS-180	B40-5017

	Engine	**Frame**
1964		
C15	C15D-101	C15-42211
SS80	C15SS-3633	C15-42211
B40	B40-5275	B40-6668
SS90	B40SS-426	B40-6668
1965		
C15	C15F-101	C15-45501
SS80	C15FSS-101	C15-45501
	C15FSS-1248 Ends	C15-49045 Ends
B40	B40F-101	B40-7775
	B40F-5275 Ends	B40-9973 Ends
SS90	B40FSS-101	B40-7775
	B40FSS-295 Ends	B40-9973 Ends
1966		
C15	C15G-101	C15-49001
C15 Sportsman	C15FSS-20001	C15-49001
B40	B40F-1149	B40-9973
B40GB(WD)	B40G-101	B40-9973
late year		
1967		
C15	C15G-101	C15G101
	C15G-2406 Ends	C15G-2406 Ends
C15 Sportsman	C15SG-101	C15SG-101
	C15SG-793 Ends	C15SG-793 Ends
B40GB(WD)	B40G-201	B40G-201
C25 Barracuda	C25-101	C25-101
B25 Starfire	C25-101	B25-101
1968		
B25	B25B-101	B25B-101
B25 (Oct)	B25C-6001	B25C-6001
1969		
B40 Rough Rider	HCB40-462M	HCB40-462M

From 1969 onwards a new coding system was adopted by BSA using (a) a two-letter prefix for month and year; (b) the model type code; and (c), the number. The latter ran from 00100 for all machines at the beginning of each production year (ie from August of the previous year) without regard for the model.

First letter month code

A January	D April	H July	N October
B February	E May	J August	P November
C March	G June	K September	X December

Second letter year code
C August 1968–July 1969
D August 1969–July 1970
E August 1970–July 1971
G August 1971–July 1972

Within those dates, the following numbers apply:

1970	**Engine**	**Frame**
B25	00272	00272

C15/B40/B25/TR25W Useful Information

Books
British Motor Cycles Since 1950 Vols 2 and 6 by Steve Wilson (PSL/Haynes)
BSA Gold Star and Other Singles by Roy Bacon (Osprey)
BSA Singles Restoration by Roy Bacon (Osprey)
Triumph Singles by Roy Bacon (Niton)
BSA Unit Singles, C15 to B50, Motorcycle Monographs No 7 by Roy Bacon (Niton)
The Book of the 250 cc BSA by Arthur Lupton (Pitmans, o/p)
BSA Singles, 250, 350, 440, 500 (Unit), Owners' Workshop Manual by Marcus Daniels (Haynes)
A selection of reprinted handbooks and parts catalogues from BMS Books, 1 Featherby Drive, Glen Parva, Leicester LE2 9NZ.
Classic Mechanics magazine Nos 32, 33 and 34 for OTJ's Tony Jones on unit gearboxes, and Nos 38, 39, 41, 42, 43, 44 and 45 for his definitive strip-and-rebuild articles on the B25. Back issues from Classic Mechanics, PO Box 500, Leicester LE99 0AA, or telephone 0858 410510.

Clubs
BSA Owners' Club, Membership Secretary Diane Jones, 44 Froxfield Road, West Leigh, Havant, Hants PO9 5PW.
Triumph Owners' Club, Membership Secretary Mrs E. Page, 101 Great Knightleys, Basildon, Essex SS15 5AN.

Shops
OTJ, The Bullyard, Rear of 83 High Street, Edenbridge, Kent TN8 5AU (Tel 0732 865683). Engine spares and services.
C and D Autos, 1193–1199 Warwick Road, Acocks Green, Birmingham B27 6BY (Tel 021 706 2901).
Vale Onslow, 104–115 Stratford Road, Birmingham 11 (Tel 021 772 2062).
MCS, 216 Leytonstone Road, London E11 (Tel 081 534 2711).
Anglo-Moto, Unit 34, Harriers Trade Centres, Hoo Road, Kidderminster, Worcs (Tel 0562 742559).
Lightning Spares, 157 Cross Street, Sale, Cheshire M33 1JW (Tel 061 969 3850).
Autocycle Engineering, Kingsley Street, Netherton, Dudley, West Midlands DY2 0QA (Tel 0384 253030).

FBS Motorcycles, Unit 5, Beauchamp Industrial Park, Watling Street, Two Gates, Tamworth, Staffs B77 5BZ (Tel 0827 251112). Late unit engine rebuilds and spares.

Jacksons, Edward Street, Chorley, Lancs (Tel 02572 64151).

Lucas Motorcycles, 50 New Street, Ross-on-Wye, Herefordshire HR9 7DA (Tel 0989 63261). Spares and replica fibreglass side panels.

Bri-Tie Motorcycles, Cwmsannan, Llanfynydd, Carmarthen, Dyfed SA32 7TQ (Tel 05584 579).

CCM, Jubilee Works, Vale Street, Bolton, Lancs (Tel 0204 385185). Late unit single and moto-cross spares.

Chapter Five

Hints and tips

Once you've selected and acquired your four-stroke (or it's acquired you), battle is joined to get and keep it on the road without rupturing your bank balance too chronically.

As emphasized in the two-stroke 'prequel' to this volume, the best single move you can make is to join the appropriate owners' club or register. If the contact addresses in this book should prove out of date, get in touch with the BMF (British Motorcyclists Federation) at Jack Wiley House, 129 Seaforth Avenue, Motspur Park, New Malden, Surrey (081 942 7914). They will have current information on all the clubs.

Club membership at around £15 per annum gets you cheap insurance with Carole Nash (see *'Useful Information'* at the end of this chapter), as well as discounts at some bike shops. Club members will help you with every aspect, and prevent the whole process from becoming a solitary ordeal.

Appropriately enough, my own outfit, the BSA Owners Club and specifically

You meet the nicest people on old bikes. This man is a chartered surveyor — honestly.

their librarian Steve Foden, has very kindly given permission for me to reproduce the following section, which concerns something that may crop up at an early stage of ownership. This is about procedures if you want to retrieve the original registration number on your old bike, which may have been lost to the DVLC while the machine was off the road and unregistered; or at least to get an 'age-related' number that's appropriate to the date of your motorbike. This is a desirable thing to do if only because in the eyes of some it enhances the machine's value, should you come to sell it on. The DVLC changed the rules about this a couple of years ago, so the information here is more up-to-date than that in the two-stroke book; and it's so clearly conveyed that I could not improve on it.

Obtaining an age-related number

'If you have any pre-1979 documentation with your motorcycle, such as dealer receipts, MOT certificates, tax discs or a photo of you as a callow youth sitting on the machine, then you stand a good chance of retaining the original number. If so you need the section on retaining the original registration.

If you don't have any documents then this is what you do.

You will need to write to the librarian who can furnish you with a machine dating certificate. He will need to know both engine and frame numbers to do this. The cost of this certificate is £2 to members and £5 to non-members.

Go and look at the numbers on the machine; it is surprising how many do not match the paperwork. If you can't find them in the normal places such as headstock or the front downtube, try the front engine mounting lug or the footrest lug on later machines. You will need to show them to the inspector later anyway. Some of the Bantam ones, in particular, are very faint so do this before you get the frame painted with 20 coats of filler paint as you may have to scrape it all off again for the inspector, to prove that they exist.

It does not matter if the machine has had an engine change provided that it is of the same generic type, eg Bantam in a Bantam frame. Problems can occur with 'bitsa' machines such as TriBsa's although the DVLA may issue an age-related number if the original frame number exists.

The recent change in the DVLA's rules means that machines which were given 'A' suffix registrations can now transfer to an age-related number; these were usually allocated as a result of a number transfer. Remember though some licensing authorities issued 'A' suffix plates in 1963 as part of normal registration procedures. If your machine has one of these plates then check with the librarian who has lists of when registration series were issued.

Also, machines which were imported and received the registration of the year, such as the imports of Saudi A65's in 1980 which received 'V' and 'W' suffix plates, can now revert to an appropriate age-related plate. New imports will be eligible for an age-related plate with a machine dating certificate.

Those machines with 'Q' are currently not eligible. However, the Club has managed to persuade the DVLA to revert to an age-related plate on occasions. If you have a machine with this plate then contact the librarian.

Take the machine dating certificate and the V5 for those machines already mentioned, to your local Vehicle Registration Office and fill in the necessary documents. The VRO will send an inspector to inspect the machine and if all is in order, a V5 with the age-related number will be issued. These plates are now non-transferable so it will not be possible to transfer them to your car or any other vehicle. It is, however, still possible to replace the age-related plate if you find sufficient documentation for the retention of the original registration mark.

Remember; as with the retention of a registration mark, the club can only advise that an age-related plate is issued. The DVLA at all times retain the right to refuse an application.

Retention of existing registration marks

When can I apply?
At any time, but the machine should be complete. Authorization to re-register cannot be given on disassembled machines.

What do I need to do?

Vehicles not registered with the DVLA
You will need to obtain the following forms from the nearest Vehicle Registration Office (VRO). See the section on local information at the front of your phone book.

Form V55/5
Form V765

If you are not intending to license the machine enter 'unlicensed' in Question 2 on form V55/5 and leave Questions 3, 4 and 11 blank.

Complete and send with the following documents:
1 Clear photographs of both sides of the machine. On the back of this photograph should be written the frame number, engine number and registration mark and signed by the applicant.
2 The old-style log book (photocopies can be accepted if they are supplied and authorized by your local VRO) or,
3 Other documentary evidence showing a direct link between the frame number and the registration mark. (See note about photocopies above).
4 Rubbings of the engine and frame numbers. This is to prevent fraudulent applications.

Vehicles registered under an age-related mark ending in SU, SV, SK, DS

Form V765 only

Complete and send with:
1 Photographs completed as above.
2 The new-style registration document (V5) bearing the age-related number.

3 The old-style log book (see note about photocopies above): or,
4 Other documentary evidence to show a direct link between the frame number and the registration mark. (See note about photocopies.)
5 Rubbings of the frame and engine numbers.

Do not send any Certificate of Insurance or fee for licensing the vehicle as they will only be returned to you. Photocopies of the old log book will only be acceptable if they are authorised copies supplied by your local Vehicle Registration Office.

What happens then?

The documents will be inspected and if they are in order then the form V765 will be completed and stamped.

For unregistered machines with an old-style log book the forms will be returned to you and you will be able to register the machine at your Vehicle Registration Office.

All other applications will be forwarded to the DVLA for them to issue a modified V5 for those with age-related numbers or a new V5 for those whose documentary evidence is seen to be adequate. When you receive the V5 you can licence the machine at the Post Office using a form V10 in the normal way.

For those machines licensed under an age-related number, a new tax disc will be issued and the old disc will have to be returned to the DVLA. Current MOT certificates will have to be sent to the DVLA to be amended.

The new registration document will show that the registration mark is *NOT* transferable to any other vehicle.

These points are important: read them

1 Making a false statement can render the applicant liable to prosecution.
2 The DVLA always retain the right to refuse an application. The club can only recommend, not instruct. Reasons for refusal will be given. However, further discussion will not be entered into. Extra evidence is support of a case can be presented at no extra cost where an application has been refused on lack of evidence grounds, but the DVLA retain the right to refuse an application.
3 The fee is non-returnable. In the event of a refusal the club will issue a dating certificate to enable an age-related number to be obtained, so be sure that the proof is sufficient before sending your application! If necessary, write first. Queries will not be answered on the telephone.
4 It is not the intention of the club to inspect all machines. However, the Club reserves the right to call for an inspection. If travelling expenses are to be incurred then you will be advised of the cost before the inspection takes place.
5 Proof of club membership is required if the reduced rate is to be applied.
6 The club can process other types of vehicles. However, it is not our intention to do so. Individual fee rates will apply along with a compulsory inspection of the vehicle. You would be advised to inspect the approved list of clubs for a more suitable organisation.

What does it cost?

£20 for BSA Owners' Club members and £25 for non-members. All correspondence and applications should be sent to Mr S Foden, BSAOC Librarian, 113 Holmville Road, Bebington, Wirral, Merseyside L63 2PX.

Left A registration like the one on this 1961 B40 would be worth winning back — especially if you were in the medical profession.

Right Unfortunately the flying helmet has had its day as motorcycle headgear. The coat looks great though.

Cheques and postal orders should be made payable to BSA Owners' Club Library Account.'

Other Clubs and registers, and indeed the largest old bike organization, the VMCC, offer a similar dating service, so contact the one appropriate to you for details.

Equipment and General

One thing you will have to get if you're starting out is a helmet. The best advice there is to buy it from a shop rather than mail order, however tempting the offers, as a good fit is literally vital, and you'd be better off verifying it personally than end up having to send helmets that don't fit back and forwards in the post. A good cheap open-face lid is the bottom-of-the-range offering from Top Tek, for £27.95 at the time of writing. One other worthwhile tip on clothing is to keep up whatever overtrousers you buy with a pair of clip-on braces, to help close the gap between jacket and overtrews. I can also mention that Argos do a very cheap bike cover for smaller machines for a little over £5. But otherwise space does not allow me to go into detail here on clothing and equipment. If you're interested, see the appropriate chapter in the two-stroke book.

Apropos that work, I must include one correction. In that book as a ploy to save money on Swarfega, I described the home-made hand cleaner you can make from mixing washing-up liquid with Ajax or a similar abrasive. This quite correctly drew down a letter from one Martin Bacon, who is an engineering manager with the job of implementing the Control of Substances Hazardous to Health (1988) regulations in his company.

So he could state with some authority that the mixture as described is positively dangerous, very corrosive and can cause eczema and severe skin cracking, with resultant oil penetration beneath the skin, and bacterial and fungal infections. Bad news, and it's no excuse for me to say that I was only thinking in terms of occasional use. Swarfega for cleaning up, plus barrier cream or proper industrial oil-resistant synthetic rubber gloves, are Mr Bacon's prescriptions. He also had another useful tip, namely to carry a pocket camera when riding, as if you're involved in any trouble on the road, it can help confirm your version of events — and has a great effect defusing belligerent drivers!

While we're on the subject of useful dodges and products, here's a few more. If you've inherited a dead battery, and particularly perhaps if you're keen to retain an original battery, don't despair. There's some magic powder from EDTA that revives defunct batteries at a very reasonable price (£1.50 last time I looked). (See *Useful Information*.) Likewise if your tank is rusty inside, Petseal is the stuff.

If it's your carburettor that needs attention, Amal themselves are still in business, or there are also some reconditioning specialists detailed at the end of this chapter. For cleaning baked-on grunge from your carb, try PDR. If your tyres need smartening, don't be tempted to use boot-polish as this is said to have a corrosive effect; get proper Carplan rubber polish from Halfords or similar. Renew inner tubes as a matter of course.

If there's no classic specialist near you and you're shopping for tyres or chain, the following may be of use. The metric equivalents which you may be offered for the old Imperial single row chains go like this:

Imperial	Metric	Imperial	Metric
$\frac{1}{2}$ x $\frac{3}{16}$	415 (though roller diameter is 0.03 in smaller than Imperial equivalent)	$\frac{1}{2}$ x $\frac{1}{4}$	420
		$\frac{1}{2}$ x $\frac{5}{16}$	428
		$\frac{5}{8}$ x $\frac{1}{4}$	520

For tyres, modern equivalents are:

	Imperial	Metric
3.10	2.50–2.75	80/90
3.60	3.00–3.25	90/90
3.50	4.10	100/90

You will probably have heard the name Loctite, for glues and fastenings, but they produce a bewildering range so it may be worth mentioning that the one most likely to be relevant for the home mechanic is their Lock 'n' Seal 242, which bonds nuts and bolts. One for a more specialized application is Loctite 290, which can cure crankcase and engine casting porosity. If you have a problem fixing push-fit exhausts into your cylinder head, PTFE sealing tape from a plumbers' merchants might do the trick.

If you can mend punctures with a compact kit and a couple of tyre irons, that's a definite asset, but you'll still need to reinflate the patched tube by the side of the road. Finilec or similar aerosols may do the job at least partially, as well as temporarily helping to seal the hole, but the sure though labour-intensive solution for inflation is a hand-pump, and the best ones for motor-cycles come off MZs; so see your local MZ stockist.

One thing your four-stroke is definitely going to need is oil, and if you use your bike as much as I hope you will, and then change the engine oil like a wise virgin every 1,000–1,500 miles, this is an item which can mount up. But bulk sizes of most good oils are available on which considerable savings can be made. It's worth looking in the *Yellow Pages* and speaking directly to the reps at wherever's nearest to you — depots for Morris', Silkolene, Penrite, etc. One of my local biking friends gets oil direct in this way, and though what he uses is admittedly non-detergent, at around £7 a gallon it's about half the forecourt price.

Then there are a few old rocker tricks that may serve you well. Use nail varnish to seal around the suspect rim of a speedometer or ammeter. If you need an instant abrasive for dodgy bulb or electrical connections, the side of a Swan Vestas packet doubles up nicely as sandpaper. To protect your chrome wheel rims (and cut down on the finger-hurting job of cleaning them), a coating of Vaseline forms a harmless protective layer that can be wiped away easily when the weather improves and you want to show off. Short lengths of rubber tubing slipped over the tyre valves protects them from knocks. Once in the saddle, it may be obvious but it's worth remembering that older machines with 6 volt electrical systems don't respond well to attempts to start them with the lights switched on. Also that no older machine, particularly a lightweight one, benefits from being kick-started regularly while on its centre stand, which will invariably twist and suffer after a short while.

One final point. If you're having work done on your old machine, I have found that reading about marque gurus, perhaps hundreds of miles from where you live, and consigning the bike to them, has been invariably disappointing; not necessarily for the quality of the work, but because doing up an old bike is an ongoing process, and if sooner or later something needs changing, adjusting or explaining, the bike and the place where the work was done are hundreds of miles apart again.

The exceptions I would make have been a couple of satisfactory major rebuilds of engines carried out by specialists, which in terms of this book would relate to OTJ for the 250/350 BSA/Triumph singles, or Jeff Tooze for LEs. But if possible, once quality of work has been established (a tricky area, but one where your local club-mates can advise you well), I would suggest you keep going to a local firm, so that both of you know the bike, and if necessary you can get it back to them without too much hassle.

Useful Information

Insurance: Carole Nash, VMCC and most one-make Club schemes, 1st Floor, Paul House, Stockport Road, Timperley, Altrincham, Cheshire WA15 7UQ (Tel 061 980 1305).

Tyres: Classic Tyres, 8 Willow Way, Coalpit Heath, Bristol BS17 2SG (Tel 0454 774903).

Armour Motor Products Ltd, 784 Wimborne Road, Moordown, Bournemouth, Dorset BH9 2HS (Tel 0202 419409).

Wheelbuilding: The Central Wheel Co, Lichfield Road, Water Orton, Birmingham B46 1NU (Tel 021 747 5175).

Alf Hagon, 350–52 High Road, Leyton, London E10 (Tel 081 539 8146/556 9200).

Electrical: M.C.E. Services, Unit 10, Ladbrook Park Industrial Estate, Miller's Road, Warwick CV34 5AJ (Tel 0926 499756). Wiring harnesses.

Merv Plastics, 201 Station Road, Beeston, Nottinghamshire NG9 2AB (Tel 0602 222783). Electrical components.

Armour (See Tyres). Harnesses, switches, components.

R.D. Components, 80–88 Derby Road, Sandiacre, Nottingham NG10 5HU (Tel 0602 491933). Authentic cotton-braided wiring harnesses.

Carburettors: IMI Amal Ltd, Holdford Road, Wilton, Birmingham B6 70S (Tel 021 356 2000). Will advise on and supply suitable Concentric replacements, jetting, etc.

Avon Engineering, Manse Brae, Avonbridge, Falkirk FK1 2LU (Tel 032486 574). Reconditioning Monoblocs.

Precision Engineering Services, PO Box 36, Saffron Walden, Essex CB11 4QE (Tel 0799 528388). Exchange reconditioned Monoblocs.

Autocycle Engineering, Kingsley Street, Netherton, Dudley, West Midlands DY2 OQA (Tel. 0384 253030). Comprehensive carb spares.

Carb cleaner: PDR from Cadulac Chemicals, R. and D. Ltd, Old Boston Trading Estate, Penny Lane, St Helens, Lancashire.

Battery reviver: EDTA Powder, K. L. Martin, 19 Brookmead, Meppershall, Shefford, Bedfordshire SG17 5SA.

Suspension units: Alf Hagon (*see* Wheelbuilding).

Armour (*see* Tyres).

Seats: R.K. Leighton, Unit 6, Gunsmith House, 50–54 Price Street, Birmingham B4 6JZ (Tel 021 359 0514). Re-covering, rebuilding or supply pattern seats.

Cables: T. Johnson (Cables) G.B., 5 Laburnum Grove, Banbury, Oxfordshire OX16 9DP (Tel 0926 651470).

Armour (*see* Tyres).

Petrol tank internal sealant: Petseal, from Autocycle (*see* Carburettors).

Cylinder head conversions for unleaded petrol: Serco, 2 Bracken Road, Brighouse, Yorkshire HD6 2HW (Tel 0484 715288).

Gaskets: T. Johnson (*see* Cables).

Armour (*see* Tyres).

Clutch plates: Surflex, Keith Blair (Tel 0283 820508) for information on nearest stockist.

Brake and clutch relining: Supreme Motorcycles, Hilltop, 1 High Street, Earl Shilton, Leicestershire LE9 7UP (Tel 0455 841133).

Horns: Taff Isaacs, 20 The Glebe, Bishopston, Swansea SA3 3JP (Tel 044128 3763).

Armour (*see* Tyres).

Sprockets: Supersprox, Station Works, Knucklas, Knighton, Powys LD7 1PN (Tel 0547 528201).

Exhausts and silencers: Toga, Rigby Close, Heathcote Industrial Estate, Warwick CV34 6TL (Tel 0926 497375) for information on nearest stockist.

Armour (*see* Tyres).

Chroming: T. Smith and Co, 35 Clerkenwell Close, London EC1 (Tel 071 253 7314).

Nuts, bolts, etc: CDS Accessories, 57 High Street, Dartford, Kent (Tel 0322-77484).

K.R. Whiston, 58 Broadhurst Street, Shaw Heath, Stockport, Cheshire SK3 8DT (Tel 061 477 8887).

Rubber (footrest, controls, kneegrips etc): Jim Hunter Engineering, 2671 Stratford Road, Hockley Heath, Solihull, West Midlands B94 5NH (Tel 0564 782122).

Armour (*see* Tyres).

Speedometers: Speedy Cables, Gaskin Street, London N5 (Tel 071 226 9228).

Speedograph Richfield, 4 Broadstone Place, Baker Street, London W1H 4AL (Tel 071 935 0402).

Vintage Rebuilds, 7 Cowbridge, Hertford SG14 1PG (Tel 0992 551713).

Transfers: VMCC Transfer Scheme, 'Arosfa', Cwmpennar, Mountain Ash, Mid-Glamorgan CF45 3DL. Will advise and supply complete sets for most old machines.

Chapter Six

True stories

As in the previous volume, we'll round off with a couple of true tales from the tarmac, as after trudging through all the boring detail and sober advice so far, you damn well deserve something a little lighter. So we kick off with...

Me and my B40

Of all the lightweights featured in these pages, the one I owned myself was a BSA B40. Buying it was a perhaps misjudged piece of theoretical business (when will he ever learn?) in that I had read in *Bike* magazine (a reasonable rag in those days) about the auctioning off of brand new B40s that had been crated up for civil defence purposes in the event of nuclear war.

Evidently the authorities had finally come to the conclusion that if someone did push the button, there wasn't going to be an awful lot of Britain left to bike about in. So over 10 years after they had been built (1965), and with the industry gone belly up in the meantime, virgin Brit singles became available again. I couldn't resist.

I say the purchase was misjudged not because the bike was a dud, but because I was in BSA mania (and funds) at the time, and already owned three other Piled Arms products: an A10 twin, a B50 unit 500 single, and a B175 Bantam two-stroke. But this didn't stop me pursuing a low-mileage (2,000 miles, in fact) example of one of the ex-CD B40s, and snagging it from a reassuringly middle-aged gent in Wooton-under-Edge for a very reasonable £230. It was a clean machine, in Land Rover green finish with AFS (Auxiliary Fire Service) stencilled in flaking red paint on the side of the tank.

The fact is that due to the other bikes, I never did put too many miles in on the B40. I had been impressed by the way it had hammered up the M4 at a steady 60 back from Wooton to North London where I was then living. On that first journey it had only faltered one heart-stopping time, and that was because, with the battery a bit low, I had started it on the Emergency switch position which the alternator electrics allowed, and forgotten to switch back to normal position once it was going OK. Luckily no damage was done.

After that the B40 lived outdoors under a cover in Highbury. Occasionally I used it for running round town, and the handling, while not encouraging

The author's 1965 B40 in AFS trim, plus the offending white tank transfers.

liberties, was perfectly acceptable. But if my then wife came along, we discovered it didn't like a pillion passenger; it was full of sound and fury from the small silencer with its flat, blasting note, but with the extra weight, signifying not very much in the acceleration stakes. Otherwise I had the A10 for touring, and the B50 for kicks — when I felt up to the battle of starting it, but that's another story. In honesty, I preferred the Bantam for riding round London, with its ultra-light weight, two-stroke squirt, complete reliability, and really excellent brakes.

The latter were not a B40 strong point. One day I was returning from my publishers, having just done the last of an absolutely final final rewrite on a crime novel of mine they were bringing out. Contrary to what you might think, finishing a book doesn't leave you elated, but rather temporarily drained and depressed. So I was moody, and attempting to crank myself up by riding a bit faster than was wise in the frustrations of London rush-hour traffic, heading north up the Farringdon Road.

I should have known better, as that particular congested thoroughfare had already brought me grief a few years before, when the Volkswagen Beetle I was sitting in just past some traffic lights had had its back bumper hooked by a Scandinavian 18-wheeler, and I had sat there helplessly as, unknown to the trucker, his juggernaut pulled my car backwards and sideways, slowly, inexorably to crunch into the side of a brand new Cortina.

That's the sort of thing which happens in the Farringdon Road, but I'd forgotten as I blatted bad-temperedly up it, with the B40 hot from over-revving, and pulled out to begin passing a grey Ford Pop. At that point, naturally, the Ford chose to make a vigorous and unsignalled right turn across both lanes, which it then couldn't complete due to traffic coming in the opposite direction. As the side of the motor flicked closer and closer in a series of slow motion frames, I gave up trying to ride round its rear end and concentrated on the anchors. The rear wheel locked, but with the front brake lever all the way back on the grip, the effect of the puny 7 in stopper was still negligible.

The rear wheel going solid meant that I was travelling sideways when I hit the Pop's back door, and like the gay conscientious objector in the First World War describing what he would do if the Huns were assaulting his sister, I (inadvertently) 'interposed myself between them' (car and bike that is). The result was a stoved-in door for the car, an extremely painful left leg for me, and only a knee-shaped dent in the left side of the tank (didn't even break the paint) and a bent footrest for the B40, which thus proved itself a tougher little number than its light appearance suggested.

That was, touch wood, the first and only time so far that I've gone down to the 'turn right, sorry mate I didn't see you' brigade. As I lay by the roadside propped up against a corrugated iron fence in considerable pain, the two low-lifes in the car alternately wheedled and blustered to get me to call it even and not involve their (probably non-existent) insurance company. The fact that

After his encounter with the Ford Popular, the author's next single was a bit heavier than the B40.

there was no real damage to the bike and that I knew I'd been going a bit fast, finally and reluctantly led me to agree with them.

A last bizarre touch was added by the fact that on an upper floor of the *Guardian* newspaper building just across the road, a journalist there who I was buying a flat from was on the phone to my solicitor discussing this when he heard the crash outside. He ran to the window to see his putative buyer sprawled full length on the tarmac of the Farringdon Road. Definitely a case of what fellow alternative journalist Royce Creasey once called The Cosmic Exchange Company working overtime.

It wasn't long after the shunt that all the BSAs (bar the Bantam, on which I went dispatching) had to go, to pay for a Norton 750 Commando. An ad in *Exchange and Mart* offering the B40 produced just one possible, a profoundly bizarre 60-year-old figure from Acton who arrived on foot in a full-length storm-coat and the rattiest pudding basin helmet I have ever seen, which he wore all the time, both off and on the bike, with the straps undone. He told us his mother had just died, as if this explained perfectly why he was buying a motorcycle.

He ignored the dent, but the deal nearly fell through due to the white BSA transfers with which I'd embellished the tank, which he didn't care for at all. Things wobbled again when we later gave him a cup of tea and some biscuits at the same time, as it seemed to be a crucial point of etiquette in Acton that you had the tea first and the biscuits separately afterwards. But in the end he paid my price and rode away on the dark green B40, and in his DR coat he looked right on it, too. The Cosmic Exchange Company in action again, no doubt.

To work on an LE

One sensation Brian Pile remembers most vividly about his LE was what happened when you hit major bumps in the road. The back end bottomed all at once and the shocks, undamped, let go right away, followed by the saddle springs, inducing a unique leaping, bouncing feeling, which was exhilarating rather than uncontrollable.

Brian acquired THO 192H, his 1969 ex-police Mk III, in 1983. He lives in Leicester, but a biking friend in London let him know about another friend's neighbour with an ex-police bike in bits which he wanted off his hands for a fiver. Since the message came via Brian's friend's wife, Brian got the impression that the bike in question was a Triumph twin, and had already reached London in his partner Linda's dilapidated Mini before he discovered that it was... an LE.

It was also in bits — three plastic bags of them, plus a heap of rusting major components. Five years previously it had been stolen from the neighbour, and before the police had recovered it, in a bizarre bid for disguise, the thieves had painted the front mudguard, headlamp and forks bright red. The neighbour had ridden it round like that for 18 months before stripping it for refurbishment and then losing momentum. He was sorry to see it go, but glad that it was to be rebuilt rather than cannibalized. Brian was somewhat embarrassed at the £5 price, which was all the man would take, particularly since all the documents were provided, in addition to a well-used owners' manual held together

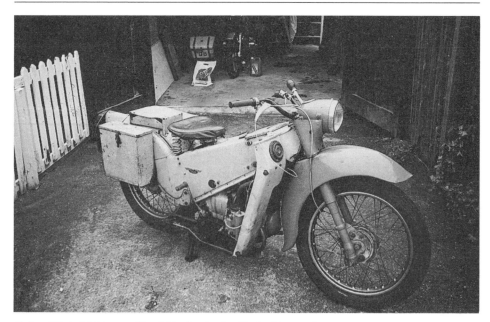

Brian Pile's 1969 ex-police LE after he had bolted it together.

with lashings of Sellotape. Brian needn't have worried. The LE's carcase was loaded into the venerable Mini, with the body strapped to the roof rack; they arrived back in Leicester safely, but when the load was removed and the Mini started again, there was a terrible graunching noise; the extra weight had final-ly demolished all four wheel bearings. So the £20 to replace them could per-haps be added to the original fiver.

Brian was in his late 20s at the time, and conformed to the LE owner profile in being rather skilled mechanically. He has built Harris-framed specials and owned and worked on a wide range of bikes, from Triumphs to a Harley, as well as several Japanese multis. Once a few months had passed and he found the time to get stuck in to the little Velo, rebuilding it proved remarkably sim-ple. No doubt this was at least partly because the engine had been running when the machine had been dismantled. It was in reasonable condition, with very few oil leaks, especially in view of the abuse it had suffered, so Brian never had to take it apart. Indicated mileage, incidentally, was 22,600 which, in view of the bike's probable 24-hour police use, almost certainly meant that it had already gone round the clock. So the good condition, even allowing for any police overhaul, was very impressive.

In Brian's garage the big lumps went together easily enough, with the only surgery necessary being to saw half an inch off the rear mudguard where it had rusted away. Otherwise, if any problems came up, help was at the other end of the phone. Brian had joined the LEOC, and on Saturday morning lie-ins he and his partner Linda derived much amusement from features in *On The LEvel*, the Club magazine, such as the woman's page with its advice on how to get oil stains out of trousers, and the proper composition of the perfect chip buttie. But for practical assistance, he had discovered an ever-obliging spares specialist, C. T. Littlejohn of Chester.

Brian off to work on the LE, which was half-way through a new paint job.

Mr Littlejohn's father, a London dealer, had bought the factory supply of LE spares when Hall Green had closed down, and when he died, Mr Littlejohn had moved north and carried on the business. Suiting the diminutive nature of the Little Engine, Mr Littlejohn's communications were all typed on the back of small invoice forms, usually for Aladdin Pink Paraffin. He was an occasionally erratic speller and typist ('speedo bable [*sic*] enclosed' 'Petrol cap (don't loose [*sic*] this one)'), but a fund of knowledge; he was also very trusting, and his prices were more than reasonable. Invoice form letters would go like this:

> The later machines only used a three-wire alternator so connect wires as colour coded and ignore the green/black one... The ignition switch has a left-hand turn for emergence [*sic*] starting but they were never any good... Make a note of wiring connections and send switch if you need new one. £8.60 each.
> Sorry, still cannot find petrol cap, keep asking.
> Your cheque for £20.85 not enclosed with your letter.

And again:

> Suggest you send the headlamp to us and we will see what we can come up with. May be able to supply new unit complete.

(He did; not new, but a second-hand unit, complete with bulbs and rim, for £8.50.) And after that:

> Thanks for reminding me about the £10, my paperwork is getting behind... The two 6 volt coils should be connect [*sic*] together, pos to neg, leaving a

pos from one coil and a neg from the other. This gives you a 12 volt system. Hope this gets you out of trouble and on the road.

Goods supplied included numerous small items, such as the ones which transformed the brakes — brake slippers and the packing shims, which as Littlejohn explained 'are placed under the slippers as required. Remind me when you next order and I will add on the price.' But they also ran to second-hand running boards, a complete new exhaust system, and petrol tank; and total bills were still under £100. About six weeks after he started, and that was just working evenings and weekends, Brian had removed the tiny sparking plugs, which took a long time as they had locked solid, poured oil down the plug holes to help free up the engine which took some hard work on the kickstart, filled up with SAE30 oil, primed the carburettor with 4-star, pulled its 'easy-start' device sideways to close the choke — and found to his delight that the LE started first kick, releasing a cloud of blue-black smoke.

Soon, after an initial hand repainting job in grey (later it would be black) the LE was ready for Brian's 15-mile journey to work at Loughborough. It was winter, and he quickly discovered that in addition to the excellent weather protection from the waist down, his feet were kept warm by the engine, even if his bottom got wet because the seat cover was shot and the saddle's padding absorbed moisture. The original heap of bits had included the police windscreen, but when Brian fitted this in pursuit of even better protection, he soon found it knocked 7 to 10 mph off the speed, so in the end preferred to remove it and wear waterproofs, because there was no speed to spare.

This was particularly true at first, when flat-out top speed was just 45 mph. Consequently Brian had the heads off and reground the valves, after which he saw a regular 50, with comfortable cruising in the mid-40s, and even 60 on occasion, downhill with the wind behind. He discovered the little bike's strengths and weaknesses by taking different routes to work, either the A50, the A6, or the flat East Midlands country roads. Purring along the latter was the most fun, including the back end bounce when you hit a hole, whereas a *fast* country road was bad news, as the LE was too slow and the other traffic too quick. By contrast in town, it was good, with the brakes adequate and the handling nimble; and the bike was *very* good during the snow and ice of a hard East Midlands winter, with poise at low speeds and a secure feeling due to the flat engine's exceptionally low centre of gravity; it probably didn't hurt that the angle of lean was restricted by the footboards, so that it could not be pushed round bends, but at the right speed it felt absolutely secure.

In the three years it carried Brian to work, there was only one major hiccup. During the first year the LE developed the well-known 'elusive misfire', and after a while, what with work and other commitments, Brian got fed up and put it into his local bike shop, who charged £80 for successfully tracing the trouble to the zener diode, mounted beneath the tank, which had been shorting out on the edge of the heat sink. Otherwise, Brian did his own maintenance, and was satisfied to discover that for setting the tappets, the version of the necessary special spanner he made himself fitted better than a bought one. He also worked out that if he reversed the tappet cover and used it to lock up the tappets so that they nipped up the C-shaped spanner, he was left with both

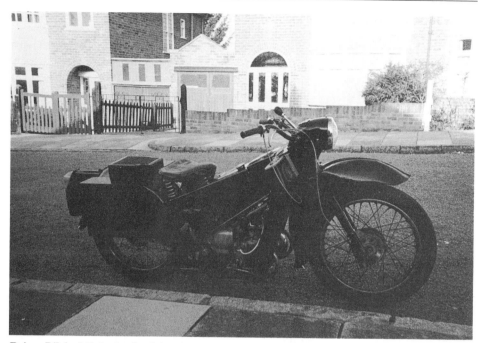

Brian Pile's LE in its final incarnation — any colour you like as long as it's black. A good commute.

hands free to do the actual adjustment. In another department it was a case of trial and error. The original speedo cable no longer worked, and after sending for one from Littlejohn, Brian spannered it tightly into position at the gearbox end. But at that position adjustment should be finger-tight only, and the cable was wrecked. Littlejohn sent another, but with a reproving 'We haven't got many of these' note.

Brian found the LE quickly developed a fan club, both at work, where it provided a bit of a contrast with his previous big Kawasaki, and locally, particularly from the garage man up the road who turned out to have a hand-change Mk I 150 stored at the back of his premises. There was only one practical drawback. Brian's LE came with the saddle and a rack for police electrical equipment, so the one time Linda ventured into town on it, a cushion had to be tied onto the rack to accommodate her. It was an amusing experience, but not repeated.

In three years, day in, day out, THO 192H added another 10,000 miles to its already considerable total. Then in 1986, pressure of other bikes finally meant that it had to go — there was a Harris-framed Laverda 1300 Mirage in the back room, and the next ride-to-work bike, a £250 Honda 500-4, with ape hangers and a bad oil leak, waiting in the garage. So the little machine was sold on, and ended up paying its way and owing Brian nothing. Sadly, Mr Littlejohn too passed away in 1988, though his nephew continued to run the business for a while, before selling the stock to the owners' club.

Brian Pile sums up the LE experience, the combination of the practical and the bizarre, as follows: 'Of all the bikes I've had — and I've liked them all —

the ones I've had most fun out of were the LE and the Harley. They were so different — and a lot of it was that people stopped and stared at you. Here was this bike that cost £5... You could charge round France on a megabike and not turn a head — but with an LE...'